ZEN MONEY BLUES

This work is based in truth, but for reasons of rhetoric and privacy, myriad details have been changed.

First Hwy 61 Press Edition, June 2009   Copyright ©2009 Hwy 61 Press

Printed in the United States
Designed by studiosignorella.com

ISBN-10: 0-9824425-0-5

ISBN-13: 978-0-9824425-0-0

ZEN MONEY BLUES

MARK BUTLER

Hwy 61 Press

For my Irish Grandmother

Zen Money Blues

The Dual Nature of Money

The ZM Types: Wiring is Wiring

The Rx of Money Mandala

I

THE
DUAL NATURE
OF MONEY

Chapter 1 Anthem

YOU GO DOWN TO N'Orleans Jazz Fest, circa 2005, a few months before the levees devastatingly break, and you see master bluesman BB King front and center on the main stage. He's 79 years old and in need of a chair, but he's not at all diminutive. Surrounding him are the members of his blues band, who by way of introduction step forward and throw down tasty licks, then step back, only to be chided by BB's "Is that all you got?" And the master bluesman is just getting started. Grinning and glinting, he turns his mischief on the audience, a happy chatty beer-drinking crowd. At the wave of BB's hand the music stops and the musicians put down their instruments. He's talking now, in that flowing Mississippi Delta meter, spelling out the terms of engagement. The blues has requirements, in case you did not know. Clapping and singing are foremost among them. While the musicians stand around, BB leans in and cups an ear toward the good folks of Jazz Fest, evaluating the singing and clapping, mostly shaking his head. Until, finally, he stops shaking his head. His eyes twinkle. He applauds the crowd. Immediately, the mood jollifies. And then—bam!—the music is on you like a thunderbolt from heaven. Like a cosmic finger in the socket. Everybody's in it, jolted, moving. Now this is the blues!

The ritual of the blues is alive and well in America, thank God. It's comprised of sneaky good storytelling and that unmistakable 12-bar jaunt. As soon as BB King starts to sing, you recognize the lay of the land. You recognize the characters, and know where the stories want to go. There is a preponderance of romantic defeats, plans gone awry, and all variety of outcomes conspiring to make you laugh. Those absurd hopes and dreams, that horrific timing, that lawman who can't stand your guts, some train tracks and some gold. You hear the blues in the comfort of first person narrative—you know, the other guy—poor boy, down on his luck, who at first doesn't really resemble you much anyway.

It is a sparkling afternoon. There is the sprawl of the Jazz Fest scene. You turn your eye back to the stage, to the master bluesman sitting on his chair. He is BB King, a black man of the South, and you are a white woman of the North, or a white man of the 'burbs, or a black man of the city, or what have you. But at some point the tables turn. His story is your story, and he's got you laughing your butt off. Aristocrat, workingman, and everyone in between: he's got you laughing at the crazy things folks do—folks like you and me.

Zen Money Blues likes this ethos. Finds it apropos the mission. For *Zen Money Blues*, too, is comprised of lively characters and itchy stories. You will recognize some of the characters, I'm confident. Yes, there will be more upper-middle-class people in these stories than you'd find in traditional blues, but blues is blues. I mean, let's be real: we humans do some pretty crazy stuff with our money. Creatively and astonishingly, we inflict all manner of wounds on ourselves and the ones we love—wounds that most of us fortunately live to laugh about. Not everyone is so lucky, of course. But *Zen Money Blues* is meant to be blues, with the full complement of humor about the human condition. After all, humor is liberation. Humor is man's best medicine. Money is important, but it's not so important that we can't laugh about it and laugh at ourselves. To my mind, it'd be glorious if, in the telling of *Zen Money Blues*, even a homeopathic dose of that BB King "look-see" humor prevails. Then there is hope, and *Zen Money Blues* is all about hope.

ZEN MONEY (ZM)

You may have picked up this book—not to read about the inimitable BB King—but because your money world isn't exactly right. Your earnings power may be as mighty as ever. Your net worth may be fine. In some cases, the numbers may be more than fine. And yet, with regard to your personal money, a substantial upgrade is in order. On some level, you already know this. It's not just about the money. There's a level of strength and clarity and balance—a yoga, if you will—that is missing. Things are more vulnerable than they should be. You intuit that, and you are right, although that doesn't make you feel any more secure. Nor does it help that, day after day, as you step out your front door, you are greeted with ordinary-Dali-esque-American surreality: the Joneses next door are trying to keep up with the Rockefellers, and even though your bullshit-o-meter is good, you cannot tell if what you are viewing is for real or a con. It's anyone's guess who has genuinely realized the American Dream and who is posing. It's hard to know how you're measuring up.

Which throws you back on your Self.

And so begins the *Zen Money Blues* journey. You start and end at a place where the personal finance gurus rarely go. You. Psyche. The Self. Your financial identity. Your true financial identity that encompasses both "the inner" (emotions, thoughts) and "the outer" (actions, results). The financial prescription to put $5,000 into your traditional IRA this year, for example, is outer. Why you did or did not follow through on that prescription, is inner. These two lines intersect at one place, and that is you. That is your personal financial identity or type, so named the Zen Money (ZM) Types. It's quite a homecoming. It's the main subject of *Zen Money Blues*.

For whatever reason, books in the personal finance mainstream chronically overlook the psyche. Cheerleading others on *(I did it; you can too!)* and crafting stern warnings *(You remember what happened to that foolish grasshopper when winter came?)* and rendering scathing judgments *(People with money problems are weak, ostentatious, missing a screw, or just plain stupid.)*— all these do not a psychological book make. The omission is puzzling. The facile treatment of psyche is puzzling. We all know how dang emotional dealing with money is. How can psyche be anything but of the first order in personal finance? What good is the medicine if the patient doesn't take it? How powerful is the truth of annually compounding returns if the investor never makes use of it? Financial prescriptions are important, don't get me wrong. Education is important. But so is the individual person. Neglecting the emotions is a bad idea. Neglecting the underlying ill-fated patterns is a bad idea. All folks are not the same. There is no one right prescription to success. What must be figured in is the human-ness of the personal financial equation. *Zen Money Blues* thus concerns itself with this. It aims to give the topic its due.

WIRING

In the realm of personal money, you and I and Uncle Murray are not all created equal. This is not bad. Differences abound in so many layers of life. Artistic folks, for example, have gifts and challenges quite apart from their scientific brethren. Same could be said for those who are emotional rocks: they have gifts quite apart from their rational/thinking type compadres. Extraverts are fearless. Introverts are contemplative. Both have their splendor, and their dicey spots. Life is a cornucopia of these sorts of qualities, differences, and trade-offs.

Self-Knowledge does not come in just one flavor either. Nor does it automatically equate to pain. In *Zen Money Blues*, it enters your world like a fine swingin' N'Orleans brass band. Somber tones of sepia are nowhere to be seen. Dr. Freud and his couch-loving avatars (The Modern Analysts) have the afternoon off. There is no need to anguish or jump into a pit of depression. This Self-Knowledge is different! It is cheerful. Tells you the rules of the personal money game. Shines a light on what you're brilliant at, and why you sometimes might be losing and leaking and even freaking. The tuba is playing now, and the bottom line is this: Many aspects of your personal money self are fixed. They're set. Wiring is wiring. You can't change it. Manage it, yes. Change it, no. Nor is everyone the same. This can produce all sorts of outcomes. Thus you will do well to have a keen eye out for your true money self, that aforementioned personal money identity (your ZM Type). That financial identity explains a lot. It cuts across all variety of socioeconomic and educational profiles.

On the *Zen Money Blues* journey, we will learn much more about ZM Typology, but for now suffice it to say that it's what makes you tick where personal money is concerned. Fortunately, cultivating the ability to spot your true money self, to see it, just isn't that hard! As mentioned, it's not about plumbing the depths of the psyche, years on end. Rather, it simply takes a little orienting. A savvy shift in perception. A fearless look in the mirror.

Indeed, flexing the brain muscle helps, and taking the ZM Type Quiz is not a bad idea either. Then you're home free. It's yours. You're good to go.

Meet Mr. Broccoli Raab. You, like I, doubtless have had more than your fair share of evenings dining out with Mr. Broccoli Raab and his wife (or your own unique version thereof). Broccoli, it should be noted, is a good guy, a manly man, possessing his own brand of charm and lovability. It's just that he also has this habit of being The Man, which he can't not do, and it consists of making a scene at restaurants, ordering items not on the menu. Broccoli raab (the vegetable, aka rapini, aka broccoli rabe, leafy, skunky, used in both Chinese and Italian cooking, and hence as utterly cool as a vegetable can get) is supreme among those items. This scene-making routine has roots. Entitlement is involved. After all, by day, Mr. Broccoli Raab is The Man. He can bloody well hunt in the world of business, and he wants a little homage when he's out on the town. He's made a lot of money. He's also a financial house afire, and it's very nearly damaged everything in his world around him. All because he doesn't see his part. He has no clear idea who he is and how he's actually behaving where his personal money is concerned. For that tiny sin alone, he may lose all that he holds dear, and that is far more than money.

Day-in, day-out this is what I see: a lot of folks running around with a case of mistaken financial identity. They are not who they think they are! Clues of this disconnect abound, at the coffee shop, in the parking lot at school, in the kitchen at a party, or in a silly spousal fight that escalates into a barbarous war. Financial advisors and planners see this all the time in the course of their work, though the "rules of relationship" with their clients render them helpless to name it. This is not therapy or self-help!

We will meet Broc again later on and will learn the details of the predicament he got himself into, and that's going to help us figure out how we can get our financial identity in line with what's actually going on with our money and our life. But before we do that, let's talk about *your* money and *your* life.

MUSINGS ON YOUR MONEY

Seeing the truth sometimes requires unlearning. So we need a teacher to prompt us a little. Enter my very proper 8th grade English teacher at Rye Middle School, Miss Herald. She'd like you to clear your desk now. It's time for a pop quiz:

> Q: True or false? How you succeed or fail, under-
> perform or outperform in regards to your personal
> finances comes down to intelligence, willpower, and
> self-discipline.
> *OK, time's up, pencils down.*
> A: False.

How you handle your personal finances has little to do with grittiness, brains, resolve and so on. No more than it has to do with having green eyes or five fingers, or being an introvert or an extravert. In order to be canny and mature in money dealings, you do not need to be a replica of pop culture's poster-child for personal finance. In reality, for the overwhelming majority of people, that's not a possibility anyway.

Evidently, Miss Herald is feeling real perky today. She feels there's more unlearning to be done, and is passing out another pop quiz:

> Q: True or false? The better you are at making money,

the more competent you are at handling your personal finances.

A: False.

Finally, it must be said that Miss Herald is also merciful. You can get it all back with the bonus question:

Q: True or false? Males with large colorful egos and outrageous incomes are the grandmasters of personal finance.

A: _____.

Well, you should read on.

At first some of this unlearning is counterintuitive. "Successful" people should be successful with their personal money, right? Except when you stop and consider how many people you've known who made scads of money, only to squander it, or slice it in two (minus 10% for taxes and attorney fees) via divorce, or just never quite resoundingly accomplish their financial objectives. Then you say, *Yes, not pretty to think about. Happens all the time.*

That it happens all the time—what's that about? And how can you keep some variation on this theme from happening to you?

ZM REPRISE

Sensing the right direction is a good start. Deftly navigating the land where money and psyche meet, however, is another story. You may have had difficulty sorting and clarifying the clash of data. Welcome to the club. Reason only goes so far. Emotions can distort. Feedback has its flaws: your friends and family who love you, might also have their own judgments and hang-ups, which further confuse the issue. Combing through family-of-origin issues is utterly confounding. "The apple doesn't fall far from the tree" may be true on a multiplicity of levels, but it doesn't mean jack (for you) that your Daddy's got The Midas Touch. It doesn't mean he failed to love you, or that he loved you too much. He has The Midas Touch and, comparatively, you feel like you've got some undiagnosed personal financial affliction. Ouch! And, not to worry! The *Zen Money Blues* journey is packed with good maps and guides and equipment and first aid, specific to this terrain of financial ID.

Of course you need focus and information and commitment, just as many planners and coaches will tell you. Everybody does. But those come after. How you ultimately handle your money has to do with what comes before—the kind of person you are before you ever write a check or pull out a credit card. It has to do with clearly seeing your "personal financial identity," getting comfortable with that financial identity even if it feels outside the bounds of who you think you are, and then putting that into action.

When you are aware of who you are financially, and have made your peace with that, you can harness its power and manage its weak spots. The point is not to change, to become something you are not. The point is to see your personal money self clearly. To get at the truth beyond any sort of self-judgment. This is tremendously powerful. Having done that, you can hire a financial advisor and know exactly how to optimize the relationship. Or, you can hire a discount broker, work your money, and not freak yourself out. Your faculty of discernment will be crisp. You'll know where you are levelheaded and you'll know where you should be suspicious of yourself. That's money. That's Zen Money. That's sane.

. . . .

Occasionally, innocence and instinct are a winning combination in the personal finance game. Ten percent of folks—Chauncy Gardener and Forrest Gump and Uncle Murray and Great Aunt Anne—walk a journey of pure unselfconsciousness, God love 'em, and it works. For them, money is like the moon. Out there. All they have to do is go out and get it, and then spend less than what they take in. Seems simple enough. Though for a select multitude, that combo is vexing, if not disastrous, and it's not because these folks can't count.

It's much more interesting than that. Grab the remote and flip to the financial channel and hear the fascinating—and somewhat damning—news story. CNBC is interviewing a research scientist from Ohio State, who shares the results of his research: there is no positive correlation between being intelligent and being rich. Yikes!

And it is exactly these "yikes" that you and *Zen Money Blues* are going to peruse, to make a study of. The money universe is not one huge undifferentiated blob. Personal money is elementally different from the money you make from your gig. Different rules, different chemistry. This distinction alone can make a heck of difference. Or, to put it in the negative: to not make this distinction can be ruinous. Can mean the world between victory and defeat, sanity and madness, smile and grimace. There is no positive correlation between being intelligent and being rich. *Zen Money Blues* says, Praise be! Let's go down that road! Let's see what that is about. It's not so bumpy. In fact, there's treasure to be found!

ANDY WARHOL'S PURSE

Meanwhile, popular culture goes in its predictable direction. Money has become entertainment and sport. Money shows and money books parade all manner of truth and sophistry, and it can be dizzying. It doesn't stop there. You go to dinner at your neighbor's house, and the dinner conversation is teeming with business deals and properties for sale and portfolio debates. It sneaks onto National Public Radio and it surely follows you to the bookstore and the airport.

It'd be nice to do something—to spiff up your finances, that is. Everyone else seems so darn tickety-boo about their cars and their houses and their get-ups and their vacations and their investment portfolios. It seems like something should bring levity and ease to this, right? You try to get your bearings. You scout around, at the personal finance section of the library or the bookstore. It's hard to feel inspired. Doubts seize you. You might even suspect you're an alien! *All this money stuff—I don't know. I'm really having my doubts.*

And you should!

The passel of literature out there on personal finance isn't for you. Look at this phenomenon a little closer, and you see that there is a strange, almost ironical self-selecting quality: it is the very people who do not need to read those books who read those books. Those folks—another 10% of the personal finance population—are not reading these books to become enlightened; they're reading them because they consume them like fuel. They love that stuff. Charts and case studies and rules of thumb and mounds of analytical data. It's what makes them run. And that's great…for them!

Pop culture may be fine for a dance party or Andy Warhol's art or conversation by the water fountain at work, but in the realm of personal finance, it is blearifying. If you tune into one of the most popular personal finance shows on TV, you'll find the host going manic over some stranger's finances. She loves a good finger wag and a mother's head shake. She's a yeller and a pontificator, and at times she is downright bombastic. It is clear that her goal is to be the super-ego of personal finance, but something else also comes through. She, and so many others like her, are desperate. And they are desperate because of this inescapable reality:

> Personal finance in popular culture is dreadfully boring. And no degree of mania, by any television personality or finance book guru, is going to change this fact.

This *ennui* is for good reason. Something is missing! People don't need to be force-fed regarding what to think. They don't find empowerment in being castigated anew. It doesn't work. It doesn't stick. People need to know who they are and how they work. Now that, in my humble opinion, is interesting. If you or the one you love has tuned out because of pop culture *ennui*, then this *Zen Money Blues* outreach message is for you all: Kindly tune back in! Efficacy matters. Effectiveness matters. Your personal money matters. Don't give up. You can't save the planet if, every day, you wake up wounded—or energetically leaking—because of your personal finances.

Which leads back to method and Self-Knowledge and the fun part. In N'Orleans (at least the N'Orleans we once knew), even a dirge would the musicians swing, eventually bringing it up to high-steppin' double time (on the way back from the cemetery to the party). Now this *Zen Money Blues* journey will be no dirge! But the method is kindred: address something challenging, address it directly, and lively it up. Thus, this slim alt-money book is infused with its fair share of wild historical and literary landscapes, and not a few subterranean anecdotes. Somehow, *Zen Money Blues* would love for you to clap your hands and sing the chorus and point and laugh, even surrender to the occasional wince. Then there's juice. You're not up in your head, lost in moral boredom or onerous "I should" lists. Your feet are on the ground. Your funny bone is working. You feel the mirthful sanity of the blues.

MONEY AND NON-MONEY

Time for a word about intention and view and fortunate circumstances and our personal finances. No one has ever accused me of being a bleeding heart but, heaven knows, the earth is struggling (as in, choking on carbons) at the present time. There are real issues here that cannot be shunted aside any longer. Finite resources, growing population, overly materialistic values, long-standing clashes of peoples and culture, all converging at a time when wisdom and compassion are still in scarce supply. There is work to be done. But just as we cannot jump over our personal psychology en route to enlightenment, so we cannot jump over the earthy reality of our money en route to healing the planet.

In the *Zen Money Blues* view of things, money consciousness should represent no more than 12.5% of our waking mindstream. It is a stream—our mind. That stream flows. If we want less than 12.5% of our consciousness on personal money, we can do that, but only if we set things up accordingly. If we don't, the whole money thing jumps out and robs us anyway, because we create myriad problems that take a lot of time to fix. If we want to spend more than 12.5% of our time pondering the many wonders of money, we should be very clear about what this generates. For some (that money-as-sport group), spending lots and lots of time focusing on money can be a delightful feast, and hence life affirming (though perhaps a bit myopic). For most, though, preoccupation with money is an abyss down which our life force flows. It is an obsession, a stream of poisonous worry, an existential fret, and we are putting all sorts of stinky negativity on our money. And the people closest to us—if not the majority of people who come into contact with us—know this. They suffer for our obsession, for our never-ending tussle with our personal money, and so do we.

Thus, I don't really believe that a book wholly and obsessively devoted to personal finance—even if its main road wends through the terrain of dark misunderstandings and a precarious Marin marriage and fragile males egos and Socrates and The Delphic Oracle and the like—is cool. And *Zen Money Blues* is meant to be cool. Not just for vanity's sake, though doubtless that plays in. Nor exclusively as an antidote to Modern Money Ennui. But for Thelonius and Miles and Dylan and Ginsberg and Ella and Billie and Janis and cool and soul and a kindred cultural universe that has nothing whatsoever to do with money—the realm of non-money, if you will. Art. Poesy. Culture. Love. Then our values are in balance. Then a book on money feels complete, responsible, and kind to the planet. Now the *Zen Money Blues* chorus can resound:

GET YOUR MONEY ROCK-STEADY,
THEN DO THE WORLD SOME GOOD.

———————

The story of *Zen Money Blues* is the story of money and non-money. It is the reminder that regardless of what we have or do not have, who we were or will be, we can be mature in our dealings and we can cherish our life, right now, this very moment. We owe it to ourselves to get our money rock-steady. What's more, the planet is counting on us.

Chapter 2 Zen and
The Modern Male Ego

REMEMBER THE AFOREMENTIONED Mr. Broccoli Raab? A good man, who hunts well in the world of business, and brings in plenty of cash. As noted, by day, Mr. Broccoli Raab is The Man. And he likes to live well. He's earned it. OK, but here's the kicker: how do you think Mr. Raab is with his personal finances—really and truly? Do you think he has what he should have, given his successes out there in the wilds of commerce? Worse: what if Mrs. Raab, bless her soul, knows best how to handle the family finances? Mrs. Raab knows best! How do you think that story is going to end?

Since I struggled through Miss Herald's test in Chapter 1, I want a chance to answer this question first:

Q: How do I think that story is going to end?
A: Rudely.

. . . .

And for this we introduce zen. Thematically, it may refer to the potency of simplicity and harmonizing, or it may refer to "skillful means" such as unsheathing the sword and cutting with ruthless compassion, because our ego or somebody or other's ego is in the way. There is precedent here, and, before continuing with our story of Mr. Raab (to be found in "The Mystery of Nine Holes and One Bullet"), I'd like to put zen in its proper context of sharp sword and ruthless compassion and skillful means.

Nowadays, zen is chic. *The golfer was really zen* ("in the zone"). *The basketball coach was really zen* (witty, inscrutable, perhaps tossed in a little paradox in the post-game interview). *The musician is so zen* (precise, in the moment, or he likes to say the word zen in his song). Some "seekers" might breeze through the carefully wrought *Zen in the Art of Archery* and be stimulated by the idea of no-idea. Take to the idea of shooting the arrow at no-target. Aim at no-target. There is the intellectual adventure of confronting paradox. But there's a hitch: You can't think your way into zen and you can't think your way out of zen. Intellect in zen is to be shot through, except when it's not to be shot through! Then there is *Zen and the Art of Motorcycle Maintenance*. This is a serious piece of narrative prose, a well-engineered treatise on rationalism and quality, well told, though by its own account it is remarkably slim on the matter of zen.

Such brushes with zen are not wrong. They certainly have their place. Nonetheless, they are domesticated. They are Siberian tigers at the Bronx Zoo. For the purposes of relating with an unruly male ego, for example, that zen will not do. Not in *Zen Money Blues* anyway. That kind of pride, the pride of the unruly male ego, is tricky and dangerous. Can be catastrophic. Though in the course of my work, there is little that I—or any financial advisor—can do with it, once it takes root in the relationship. Unsheathing the sword is not appropriate. This is financial planning, not psychotherapy! But in *Zen Money Blues*, you sharpen the sword and go for it. You are not the first. You are not alone. Zen has a long line of impeccable though undeniably eccentric characters.

Consider Rinzai (aka Master Lin Chi). He was the ninth-century Chinese patriarch, who left his appellation to one of the two major schools of zen. He was a bad ass. He was rude and ill-tempered. His methods of assisting his students included yelling, slapping, smacking, and generally not being helpful at all. Folks can chuckle about it now, but I assure you that you would not have wanted to be in his monastery back when: there were definitely easier ways to put rice in your stomach.

Some years back I was at a Rinzai-style zen temple in New York and a student asked the teacher what would happen to an asshole if that asshole attained enlightenment. The teacher flashed red with irritation, seemed to mutter "asshole" while glaring at the student, then said quickly, "He'd become an enlightened asshole… obviously."

Which brings this story back to zen and the modern male ego. I dwell there, not because today I'm in a strong anti-male Oedipal phase, but because this alpha male style will assuredly have a violent allergic reaction to Miss Herald's next lesson. A lesson of unlearning. A lesson of discernment. A lesson so everyday-ordinary it is easy to overlook. Some folks grok it immediately. Others just don't see it. They can only see their preconceptions, like looking at the famous perceptual illusion of the 1888 postcard of the old lady and the young girl. Which one is it? They can only see the old lady OR the young girl, not both, till you point it out. Hence, unlearning is necessary. Unlearning is how we shed those preconceptions. Unlearning is how we orient ourselves anew. Money isn't what we think it is. In fact, it is not static at all. It is not always the same. Nor are we. Money at home is radically different than money in the world. The rules are different. Mastery in one realm does not automatically lead to mastery in the other. And for that, sword in hand, we will return to Mr. and Mrs. Broccoli Raab, our teetering Marin couple, and "The Mystery of Nine Holes and One Bullet."

Chapter 3 The Mystery of
Nine Holes and One Bullet

F IRST OFF, I'D LIKE to reverse course and ask that you engender a little sympathy for Old Broc. His foibles are human, indeed, and could be yours or mine. Besides, as you will see, he's going to make matters worse for himself. And I, as financial advisor, prove to be little help, commencing work with him and his wife in the middle of their years-on struggle. A subterranean struggle, I might add, which I never anticipated, though a blow-by-blow (or should I say, throw-by-throw) account was provided to me later, whereupon I at least made myself useful by taking notes for this—Miss Herald's first case study. So, without further ado, it's time to hit the road, take The Inner Highway 61 north and turn left at Vicksburg, with final destination none other than the American Tuscany—which is to say, Northern California.

• CASE 1 •

BACKGROUND: For both Broc (David) and Mrs. Broc (Jana), this is a second marriage, entering year 16. They have one child (daughter, 13) between them, and kids from previous marriages, who are grown up and out of the house. In the go-go years Broc and Mrs. Broc made great coin, knew how to live large, then got soft on the income side and sloppy on the spending side. Now they aspire to get back to a more stable, solid groove. Or so they say when I begin to work with them. However, it seems likely they never had a stable, solid groove. It wasn't necessary. Now, like a slew of their peers circa 2004, they are house rich and cash poor.

PERSONALITIES: Broc is alpha dog, and a bit hyper, but when he takes some of the edge off, he's a super-fun guy, looking to join a pickup game of ultimate frisbee at the park with the 20-some-things, or ready to blaze into the city and hear some obscure singer-songwriter at the Great American Music Hall, or convinced that this is the moment to open four great bottles of Pinot for a tasting on his deck, where you take in the kingly views of the hills and the bay and San Francisco. He's Type A, West Coast style.

Gigwise, Broc has been an intrepid buyer in the soft goods market, importing goods from China, Korea, Malaysia, and Indonesia. From cheap sunglasses to rayon shirts to baby shoes, he monopolized niche markets and delivered goods for the right price to a few big box retailers. He had his formula and he knew how to get paid. In the years before working with him, I knew him socially, through a mutual friend, who knew the Broccoli Raab routine, and who knew the general numbers of Broc's gig; and that friend guessed that Broc made about 300-500K a year for ten years running. Later, Broc confirmed these numbers. Unfortunately, when Broc and Jana commenced work with me, he was in the midst of a long "sabbatical" (approaching two years), and the soft goods import game was changing quicker than mercury.

Jana, heretofore known (unfairly) as Mrs. Broc, is the heroine of this story. The move she made was risky, as we shall see. It was born of a cold brilliant fury, potentially escalating the matter to the point of no return, though Rinzai might have approved. With one quiet sharp sting, she set something in motion that was able to blow holes in that strange volatile psychic armor known as The Male Ego—and she even received an 80% sincere apology from Broc for mucking things up all these years. Now I don't mean to mess with the suspense of the story, but, unlike the sunny, extraverted Broc, you might want to know what lies beneath for Jana (hint: Scorpion).

In more favorable times, Jana smiles at Broc's craziness. He blazes and she is cool like the moon, and they love each other. Socially, she is fun to talk books and writers with, though she has that mischievous knack of getting you to talk too much about yourself: your spouse, the kids, your golf game, or your rant *du jour*. Whereas Broc is the epitome of activity, she is stillness and clarity, and wins your heart with a kind note or kicky voicemail. In her professional work as an environmental lawyer, all these qualities must have made her a magnet for business. In recent years, however, the family decision was for her to be a stay-at-home Mom, doing only the occasional gig here and there, and more often than not taking on sundry projects in the not-for-profit world.

It was Jana who insisted that we three work together in a financial planning capacity. There was a run of several "getting going" meetings, and all the elements (for trouble) were there. Broc had this disconcerting habit of talking about "his" money. This was an inaccuracy. The wealth was unequivocally theirs, not his; it had been commingled and co-created and co-spent every step of the way. In the meetings, he was a mess. Flights of pride about income that once was, and plunging bewilderment that after home and retirement assets, there were not a whole lot of funds left in that taxable account.

We spent it, pierced Jana.

Broc wasn't in listen mode. He rarely is. For all her non-verbal intensity, punctuated by the occasional barb, Jana did not challenge Broc. Maybe she thought occupying the passenger seat was the best modus operandi for this marriage. Whatever the case, it was a waste. Her instincts around personal finances were excellent. She communicated a sharp, practical mind that pin points problems and thinks in terms of solutions. The discussions were critical. Because of money, their marriage was in obvious jeopardy. Sadly, though, Jana never pressed it here. They'd get to the critical spot, the moment of truth about their financial situation, which would mean someone or something would have to take responsibility and change, and then inertia would take over.

Time would reveal why. I had been too hard on Jana. She had legitimate grounds for her reluctance. Broc was trouble. Intensifying the personal finance discussion was, as I experienced first hand, a trigger for neurotic attacks. Not only was Broc dreadfully emotional, but he was in complete denial that he's dreadfully emotional. *Don't tell me: I know money! In my good years, I printed money. I know my money better than anyone. Look at the deal I got on this house. The appreciation on this beats the heck out of any stock market returns. But now you're telling me that I can't touch my IRA-rollover or Jana's SEP because of taxes and penalties, and that if I don't take that crap job they offered me, wasting my time for peanuts, then we should sell this house and get something smaller?*

I held my ground in silence. That was the right thing to do. That was the only thing to do. Jana looked embarrassed, and furious.

Zen Money Blues—a safe literary alter ego—would never have held its tongue. It would have said: *Broc, you're crocked. You've* *had a stranglehold on the personal family finances and look where it's gotten you. Drop the imperious male ego thing. It isn't working! Get out of the way. Your ability to make money is something utterly different from your ability to handle money once it's come home. Some people can do both. You can't. End of story. Humble yourself to this first essential truth of Zen Money Blues: **making money and handling money are two very different things.** Respect this truth or you're going to hurt yourself and the people you love.*

But *Zen Money Blues* was not living and breathing then. Thus, Nature took its course. And Broc mulled and brooded, and in the end did resign himself to the fact that they were house rich and cash poor, and he agreed with Jana that downsizing while actively looking for the right gig was better than staying there and taking on the wrong gig.

Or so we all thought for a number of months, till good news spoiled the party.

Literally. The day after the party, I got to be a part of the bad hangover, receiving a bevy of wild emails. Here's a sketch of what transpired.

ACTION: Belvedere, CA (6:00am)—In their Tuscan style home, not far from Jerry Garcia's old hilltop pad. They are in the kitchen, leaning against marble topped counters, waiting on the gurgling coffee maker. The kitchen's a mess from having hosted company the night before, a cheerful evening turned to hell right about the time that beverages and crudités were served. "Good news" was the spoiler. Their real estate agent had phoned; a bona fide cash offer was in hand for their home, coming in well above asking price. And Broc whispered flat out: *Nope. Not doing it.* Jana fell into a cold fury. Held that fury till the last guest was gone and it was time to tidy up the kitchen. Then they went at it. And got nowhere, except they woke up their daughter, who told them to go to bed. And they did, leaving a kitchen full of plates and containers with chicken and collards and mashed potatoes and wine bottles. By all accounts, they slept like hell, and awoke in a grim state of mind.

"I don't care, " said Broc, trying to get breakfast and then escape to Meadow Club, in search of a crack o' dawn golf game. "I changed my mind. I don't want to sell. There's nothing more to discuss."

Jana was unmoved.

"You can't make me sell. That's all there is to it. We bought this house with the money I made."

She stoned him in silence.

"So we're in a little financial shit," he said, "and all you can think about is: me, me, me."

He was looking for his new golf visor, checked to make sure he had keys and wallet, and he could not be gone fast enough. The drive over to Meadow Club was mellow, uneventful, and while there was no pickup game to be found, Broc thoroughly enjoyed the brisk morning air and the fact that there was no cell phone reception in that hollow. As he finished number nine, he even felt that he was getting his groove back, and that felt particularly auspicious. He was trying to figure out what betting game he should play against himself when he pulled the 77% organic XOXO chocolate from his golf bag. He loved this tiramisù that Jana always packed in his bag for the back nine. Perfect tiramisù. Though this one had a note attached to it, folded in two, held down by the fat purple rubber band that kept the broccoli stalks together.

The note read thus:

THE INSANITY IS OVER. GIVE ME THE PURSE
OR DON'T COME HOME. – J
P.S. THE LOCKS ARE ALREADY CHANGED BY NOW.

What happened next is a bit of a one-man crime scene, wherein accounts change according to Broc's levity and relish for storytelling, since he was the only witness, save the greenskeepers and mowers, who did not speak English. For, it has been told, there was the din of battle that morning, as Broc went on an epic club-throwing club-banging rampage, on each and every hole, on his way to the most miserable nine holes of golf he had ever and probably would ever play. And near the end of it, when exhaustion took him and he slipped on some wet leaves and landed on his ass, he broke down and bawled, and thought about a few things, like how much he loved Jana and their daughter, and bawled some more, till one of the golf shop boys came out looking for him, worried that he'd had a heart attack or something, so long was he taking to play the last three holes. Old Broc—what a sight he must have been. The man least likely to commune with quiet and nature, right there, kind-of sort-of communing with nature, and, dare I say it, getting in touch with his soft emotional side. OK, forget that last comment, but suffice it to say: Jana had moxie, and a wee dram of luck. At the exact perfect time, she levered all the good will and love she'd been storing up all these years, and she moved her man off the dime. Got him to change. And, while I'm not much of a betting man, one thing is for sure: the odds were against her. Then again, no one knew Jana could shoot nine holes with one bullet.

Chapter 4 Hunter Money vs. Hearth Money: Making the Mission-Critical Distinction

IF *ZEN MONEY BLUES* wore glasses, they'd be bifocals. What we call "money" in fact has two separate, very different realities—with different rules and norms, as different as near and far, night and day, sun and moon, home and office. We need the right pair of glasses to see this money world in its elemental parts and in its entirety. The glasses need to be used correctly. Looking at personal money through the "hunter's" lens will delude and deceive, which is what happened to Old Broc. He did know how to make money, just not how to manage it once he had it. It never dawned on him there was a distinction to be made. It never dawned on him he needed to see the line that separates home money (personal finance) from work money (active wealth accumulation).

Let's pause here and put into place definitions and descriptions of this yin/yang money universe. Through one lens we will see money as "Hunter Money"—your work, your active pursuit of wealth. Through the other lens we will see money as "Hearth Money"—your wealth in hand, regardless of how it came to be (inheritance, business dealings, divorce, marriage...). Success on the *Zen Money Blues* road depends on making this Hunter/

Hearth Money discernment. So, buckle up, and please pass the bifocals.

Hunter Money is active. It's the money you make out there, in the world. The aim is to generate wealth, to kill the elephant or wild boar or rabbit, to pan the gold, to ink the deal, to land the new client—to acquire "money" through your active works. In a word, Yang! On the 1040 tax form, the Internal Revenue Service asks: Are you actively involved in the operations of this business? *Yes* means earned income. *Yes* denotes Hunter activity. For the purposes of this book, we will keep profiles of Hunters at this very basic level— encountering a few conspicuous hunter characters along the way.

Hearth Money is our chief concern. Of course, as the opposite of Hunter Money, this term could also be called "personal money." Yin money. It is the money in your pocket. When you kill the wild boar, you don't actually eat it then and there. You bring it home. Same with your money. You don't eat your money at the office. It needs to be converted, processed, cooked, spiced up. Actually, eating the pig raw is probably kind of dangerous. Will make you sick. But enough of the analogy. The point is that Hearth Money has its rules and requirements, and there is a primary internal component. Your psychology. Your Hearth Money Type, aka your Zen Money (ZM) Type. See that clearly, align with that energy, and there is no doubt you will have more health, energy, and focus to make your way in the world, be that for more money, fun, generosity, healing, or peace.

THE DUAL NATURE OF MONEY

Like a coin, money has two sides. Heads and tails, hunter and hearth. You do your thing "out there" and you come home, bringing your earnings with you. The very moment that money crosses the threshold of home and hearth, the moment that money leaves the company coffers (i.e., you get paid) and hits your personal checking account—something happens and the rules change. Money flips, from heads to tails, and so does your financial self. Spontaneously. Simultaneously. Alchemically. It doesn't matter why. That money is now personal money. That money, if you will, is no longer Hunter Money. You're home. You're not hunting. You're breathing out. You are now in the personal money universe. Go out to dinner: Hearth Money. Go to Whole Foods: Hearth Money. Go to Nordstrom: Hearth Money. Go to the café: Hearth Money. Go to the CD shop: Hearth Money. Give your teenager 20 bucks: Hearth Money. Give to your church: Hearth Money. Buy a round of drinks: Hearth Money. Pay your bills: Hearth Money.

Something happens and the rules and identities change. What matters is that you recognize the cosmic game afoot, that you make the connection. Hearth Money has its own rules and its own archetypal characters (the ZM Types—more on this soon enough). Hunter performance does not shed light, good or bad, on your Hearth Money identity. The book *The Millionaire Next Door* is an excellent case in point. It is rife with stories of middle-class people who did nothing flashy. Label them stereotypical rabbit hunters in the Hunter Money realm. Plumbers, grocers, auctioneers, electricians, teachers, insurance agents. No matter. They socked away a little bit, month over month, year over year, and in the afternoon of their life found themselves in a very positive (personal) financial position.

Intuitively and empirically, many of you already know the truth of the Hunter/Hearth Money dynamic. You don't have to extend your mind's reach too far to recall a family member or friend or business companion who made oodles of cash in business and had an unfortunate knack for squandering it: investing in restaurants that went belly up, quitting his or her day job and *voila!* becoming a day trader, spending blindly amidst a marriage-gone-bad and then not being able to afford to get divorced (and live in the same high style) when it was time to move on. Or the more mundane version of this: good folks, talented and hard working and well paid, who get down the road of life and don't seem to have nearly as much as they should have. A miscue here and there, costly though not catastrophic, and then multiply it by the lost time value of money, and these middling miscues leave their mark. Their modus operandi was based on the undifferentiated view of money. Regarding this matter, *Zen Money Blues* is intense: **When in the hunter realm, do Hunter Money; when in the hearth realm, do Hearth Money. Know the difference; don't mix the two.**

DOCTOR IN THE HOUSE?

It does not require intelligence or education to make this Hearth/Hunter Money distinction, just unlearning. Take doctors, for instance. They are notorious in this regard. Their professional training and sense of professional self (hunter realm) is inculcated with a strong feeling of leadership and self-confidence and judgment. This is a good thing. You don't want your surgeon waffling with the knife in her hand. You don't want her asking the nurses if it is OK with them to get her the tools she needs. A dear friend (and surgeon) even adds a bit of self-deprecation to the equation, with his medical school maxim: *Doctors—we're seldom right, but never in doubt!*

Apply that approach to personal money and investment, and this can be a truly bizarre cocktail. During the raging dot-com years of '98-'99, I had a client, Leo, who was a young star of cardiology down in Denver. Leo liked voicemail. Once a month, always on a Monday morning, I'd come into the office, and the green voicemail light would be on. Waiting for me would be a three-minute message (the max you could leave). It was a list of everything Leo was thinking about, based on his research and sundry ruminations: penny stocks he thought the world of; ideas for selling what was low and ideas for buying what was selling high (last year's winners); and countless ideas for stop-sells and buy-limit orders. He hated downside volatility (namely, his portfolio going down with the markets) and yet he equally bemoaned the steady returns that his "value-oriented" portfolio delivered. It was the voicemail from hell. It was as if the plan we had carefully crafted, based on his risk tolerance and stated objectives, was beside the point. Making that investment plan was "our" job. Implementing that plan was "my" job. It was clear as day: it was time for Leo to follow. That's why he hired me. Instead, he wanted to lead. The Sunday voicemail was his mercurial paradise, guaranteeing one-way communication, devoid of any irritating questioning or diverging counsel from me. Leo did not want a professional investment advisor. He wanted obedience and adulation. Duration, you can imagine, would not prove to be one of the qualities of this relationship.

But first, it got stranger. The dot-com investment universe was rising parabolically, and this was killing Leo. He began to send me—"for my review"—different business plans for start-ups that he had fallen in love with. Two I recall vividly: one was a company that had come up with a less bruising way to do liposuction and the other was a software game that taught you how to play the piano on the computer. Now the concepts seemed interesting enough, but the quality of information and transparency were insufficient. In the best of circumstances, these are the riskiest of the risky investments. Leo had an OK family balance sheet, but he definitely did not have 50K to throw at each investment and lose ALL. The rule of thumb on any investing and diversification plan is this: never lose more than 1% of your total investable assets to a given investment. Losing 100K was more than 1% of Leo's investable assets, by a considerable margin. Actually it was closer to 10%, and the loss that ensued was a crying shame.

What worked so well for Leo as a cardiologist was a huge detriment when it came to his personal investments. I doubt it was even a conscious application. My hypothesis is that he was on autopilot, which might have sounded something like this in his head: *pushing and directing and leading and making snap judgments has done me well—awfully well—in my medical practice; it's saved lives and it's made me the success I am; and now I apply that approach to my money.* Of course, simple math and logic tell us that even a super-bright guy like Leo will probably do much better at the activity that takes up 200 hours per month versus the activity that takes 2 hours per month. The hubris itself is not outlandish, but the resulting blindspot is troublesome, and could be quite expensive.

THE ORIGINAL WISE GUY

You may recall this fallacy of "overreaching," which has roots in the Ancient World. Socrates then was the gadfly *nonpareil.* Not known for his good looks, he asked more questions than Perry Mason and ended up infuriating the powers that be, who escorted him out of the party early, requiring him to swill several shots of hemlock. In the *Apologia* (recounted by Plato) he locks on to this very fallacy of overreaching, while pretending that the point of his journey through Athens is to prove the Oracle at Delphi wrong. For the Oracle cannot be correct: *Surely I—little old Socrates—cannot be the wisest man in all of Athens.* Thus he goes to the noble statesman, the blacksmith, the poet—all masters in their fields—and inquires of their breadth and depth of knowledge. What he finds is that all of these men, while masters of their chosen field, make a leap of folly, make a leap of self-intoxication, a leap which Socrates himself deems unwise and unfounded: they assume that because they hold special knowledge in their field, they therefore hold special knowledge of many other things, including metaphysics and the universe. The blacksmith is confident that his knowledge of blacksmithery naturally translates to understanding matters of math and wisdom and relationship and the quintessence of the universe. The other stories follow a similar track. Disappointed, Socrates concedes defeat to the Oracle: he accepts the label of "wisest man in Athens" only because he knows that he does not know.

Successful hunters are prone to a variation on this theme of overreaching—of not making "the distinction." They know how to go out and make money. They know how to accumulate the good stuff and bring it home. They have pride. They should have pride. They have confidence. Skill. Mastery. Cocksureness. As noted, some stalk elephants, wild boar, tigers, bears; others hunt rabbits, birds, and small game. Who they are, what they habitually seek: that defines them out there, in the martial world of gathering wealth, plundering wealth, actively generating wealth. That identity and activity is their Hunter self. It describes how they actively gather money out there. But that is only half the story. Money has this other side (Hearth). Being good at one is no indicator of being good at the other. Neighbors, friends, family, celebs—there's a bevy of whispered and broadcasted stories that corroborate this.

MYTHIC ROOTS

When we reflect on these stories of underwhelming out-comes—stories that are both fresh and extend back to the Great Depression—we recognize the veracity of money's dual nature. We make the distinction. Success at the outside game has no correlation to success at the inside game. It's as if different DNA and different cells are employed for each activity, only Mom and Dad and Grandma and Grandpa forgot to tell us this. Or did they? My wild speculation is that for thousands of years, the oft-fantasized village of our forebears had very clear practices around division of labor and how to handle profits. The mythic village functioned in a self-selecting manner. Those who were good at hunting hunted, and those who were good at hearth matters handled the hearth. If you ruined the barbecue or tanned the animal skins improperly, regardless of how good a hunter you were, that probably meant you ended up with other domestic tasks. Or the village got weak, hungry, cold and died out over time. My wild speculation is that distinguishing hunter skills from hearth skills wasn't necessary, because it was automatic in the social fabric of how the village and its leaders took care of themselves. Evaluating hunter prowess and hearth "wiring" were both social matters, and hence regulated socially.

Clearly, I am no Jared Diamond. But it does seem to make sense that the modern world demands our attention on this matter. Gone is the mythic village. Gone too is its microcosm, the multi-generational family. What a safety net the extended family was for many of us! Gone. In its stead, the modern world gives us unprecedented mobility and fierce individualism, and a whole new set of responsibilities and complex equations. Money, it appears, is one of them.

It's funny that we prepare our whole young lives to be capable hunters, repeatedly clarifying where we shine and where we're not so special; working hard as an undergrad at university, perhaps grunting up the steep hill of professional school; doing the necessary internships or apprenticeships, and then working our way up from newbie to legitimate player—yet there is an infinitesimal amount of energy and education allocated to personal finance. To who we are (our personal financial identity). To qualitatively and quantitatively making the most out of what we earn. Implicit is that personal finance just isn't that hard. On the face of it, this is true. It's not that hard. But it is complicated. Because we humans are complicated. The fullness of our humanity does not go away, even in these modern times. Money—particularly personal money—has become a terribly private affair. As Freud noted a hundred years ago, *Money is as taboo as sex.*[1] This further complicates matters. In the mythic village, they'd honor you as great warrior/hunter and at meal-prep time they'd ban you from the kitchen. No such self-regulation occurs in modern times. No uncle tells you to stop being a fool and start handing over your paycheck to your spouse. There's good reason that so many obsess about money. The individual stakes are very high.

The *Zen Money Blues* journey really gets going here, by making this mission-critical distinction of money's dual nature. Hunter Money and Hearth Money. Yang and yin. Work and home. Once you recognize money's dual nature—acknowledge this alchemical progression of mind and money—you are poised to shine a light on your Zen Money (ZM) Type, your personal financial identity. Much of that identity is fixed, and knowable, and very useful to have ready to hand. For then you know when to lead and when to follow. When to be private and when to be social about managing your finances. When it's working and when you need a skillful helping hand. The Elephant Hunter, whose beguiling story is right around the corner, could have used just such a helping hand. He was a great hunter, he knew. But the rest was unwieldy. He suspected there was something going on with money's dual nature, and he was open to assistance from others. For Leo the Doctor, not so much. Unlearning was not possible. Relinquishing some control was unimaginable. In the personal financial realm, Leo's prognosis seemed to be one of continued misadventure.

To be sure, there are folks who have superb ideas and fine sensibility. They might even bring smart deals and players to the table, and this is exciting and fun. But they do this with an element of non-attachment: nothing has to work! *Let's knock it around. Sit with it a while. See what it tells us. See how it fits into our overall strategy and objectives.* Good judgment is born of such process. Regarding the case of Leo the Doctor, it's not that he was wrong and I was right. It was that Leo was NOT one of those people with excellent, dispassionate ideas or terrific private equity connections. He was wandering through the personal finance terrain and he was lost, not aligned with his financial identity. Thus his actions and ideas were odd, jarring. He believed all his thoughts. The results, well, they spoke for themselves.

In closing, it may come as no surprise to you that "old money" families often display an uncanny knack for 1) already putting into practice the Hunter/Hearth Money distinction and 2) intuiting their ZM Types (that fixed identity of strengths and weakness, in relation to their personal family money). Though tempting, I'll spare you the grand speculation on why this old money dynamic is so, and simply proffer this social Darwinism: old money families have had generations to work out the kinks, and the best of those families has never hesitated to pass wealth along via trusts, for example, which by their very nature have the social construct of trustees (savvy, prudent individuals and advisors) and code (law, trust, vision, guidance, intent)—a kind of modern village! If Johnny III was a brilliant Yale-schooled esquire (hunter realm) and still a little too wild in his early 30's—the word that comes to mind is spendthrift—then things were set up by family and counselors so that it was easy for him to make the small financial mistakes but not the big ones. Like it or not, his personal finances were managed for him, and later in life, assuming he wasn't embittered and resentful about it, he'd be likely to do the same for his children, albeit with essential refinements. Most folks, however, are not beneficiaries of generations of working out the kinks. Take the Elephant Hunter. He is of excellent pedigree, though not generations of family wealth. You'd like the Elephant Hunter if you met him. He's a very cool guy, whose money innocence comes to the fore at a strange time in his life. The Hunter/Hearth Money distinction is the natural bridge to exploring the ZM Types. The Elephant Hunter fell asleep and woke up on that bridge. His is a story of the unexpected, and partial redemption.

Chapter 5 The Elephant Hunter's Homecoming

I T APPEARS THAT WHILE The Elephant Hunter was stalking world markets and positioning himself to get paid up the wazoo, something dark and unconscious was afoot at home. His personal family money—the money he'd already accumulated from previous kills—was left in the wrong hands. These were the gross and subtle entanglements of a very busy man, on autopilot with his money. This is his story. It is a reminder of the stakes of the game. For the mistakes the Elephant Hunter makes with his personal money he would not in a million years make in business. And the damage done touched more than money.

• CASE 2 •

INTRO: History tells us that homecomings are not as peachy as we'd like to think. No doubt for reasons of her own, Mother Nature likes to make us forget these stories. Agamemnon—King of Kings—after ten years of war, had a most unfortunate and stinging homecoming. Odysseus—the great tactician and king— gone for ten years fighting alongside and under Agamemnon, did not have the smoothest of rides home either. Enduring and overcoming one epic detour after another, he must have been wizened like a prune by the time he returned home, though he did rejoin his Queen, who was good and true. Then there is Taylor. He is the Elephant Hunter. He is a thoroughly modern man, noble in his own right, who stalked world markets, and met with his own perils upon coming home. This is his story.

BACKGROUND AND CHARACTER PROFILE: Taylor is the Elephant Hunter and he lives in the hills. His home is an unpretentious pad on a kingly spot overlooking town, with expansive views of mountains and plains. His path to wealth accumulation relied heavily on what has become an uncommon art: astute observation of others. The vessel of his mind captures and records the smell and feel and sweaty palms of a business interaction. His cultivated strengths more than compensate for his lifelong struggle with dyslexia. In the world of M&A—site of his first two big kills—he had a talent for sniffing out fear, for understanding the unsaid, for uncovering value and making the pie bigger, and then pressing for the advantage. His genuine simpatico never hurt him. In the end, he wrought deals that got everyone a nice piece, and no one begrudged him his handsome payout.

CLIMATE: It was the summer of 2002 and the stock markets were roiling. The last half of 2000 and much of 2001 had been punky. Then came the September 11 destruction—very, very painful. Everyone was reeling. On the financial front, the fallout was predictable, for a while anyway, until the markets about-faced and rallied. The fourth quarter of '01 ended on a hopeful note. 2002 rode that feeling with a cheerful song of unanimity: *the economy and markets would rebound "robustly" in the first half—it had to be!* But when this did not materialize, a violent July to August

(2002) decline followed, and the proxy for the equity markets—the S&P 500 index—was worth a disquieting 24% less. Enron had imploded. WorldCom had imploded. AOL had exploded. Tyco was a disgrace. Scary as all that was, the real carnage was in the Nasdaq, which hit 1,200—a smooth 76% below its March 2000 high of 5,000 plus.

ACTION: In that summer of 2002, Taylor, our Elephant Hunter, was bringing to the ground his biggest kill yet. Eighteen months prior, his company—one that he himself bought into and helped turn around—had been acquired with stock by a publicly traded media conglomerate. Buoyed by the leadership of the charismatic Barry Diller, this media conglomerate was somehow still a darling on Wall Street. Perhaps the last darling, whose darlingness could expire at any moment. Which would not be good for Taylor. Along with the stock, he had received a ginormous amount of performance-based options in the new company, tied directly to his contribution to the company's bottom line. If he met or exceeded expectations, Taylor stood to earn a massive payout. All he had to do was go on a binge of acquisitions that would immediately add to company earnings. Vet through the wreckage that was the public markets and find unloved quality companies and buy, buy, buy. Which brings up another essential piece. That ginormous quantity of performance-based options wasn't good forever. The clock was ticking. Deliver earnings to the company NOW or go home with no elephant.

With his unflinching style, Taylor delivered. In 18 maniacal months of due diligence and acquisition, he made his new company proud, and more valuable. And the love went both ways. With heart a-pounding, and the company stock price holding on for dear life, Taylor was granted his options and he immediately cashed out. A rich man already, our Elephant Hunter came home a significantly richer man.

At least he thought he did.

REDUX: Let's go split screen and re-view 2002. For years Taylor also ran a hedge fund with a nice slice of his own family money. He traded currencies and options contracts and thinly traded micro-cap stocks and IPO's on various small world stock exchanges, much of it through a nifty arrangement with Goldman Sachs. His trading systems were enhanced and refined from his formative years working at another hedge fund. This was no dabbling in day trading. It was a formal business. Taylor actively ran it. This was Hunter Money.

In 2001 he called into the business Little Cuz, a convivial sort for whom Taylor had great fondness. Taylor needed to be smart about his time, and negotiations were perking along with the aforementioned media conglomerate. He needed someone he could trust, someone who was smart, someone who could work the system, someone who would follow orders, while he focused on his next kill. Cuz, by now a young man of 32, seemed to fit that bill; was perhaps a little thin on the experience side of things. But Taylor did his best to break him in. Besides, Little Cuz was family. If you can't trust your family, whom can you trust.

Right?

Fast forward to the summer of 2002 and the markets were pitching, nauseatingly so. Little Cuz was at the helm and Taylor was nowhere to be seen, long since gone on the hunt. In fact, Taylor had not been around in months. There had been the occasional check-in phone call but somehow the keen observer, the keen listener, the master of due diligence and the deal, was not engaging. I speak of our Elephant Hunter. He could not afford distraction. Time was not on his side. The sirens were ubiquitous. Coming home empty-handed was more than a plausible scenario. The hunt was reaching its climax.

In retrospect the warning signs had been clear as Carmel in October. Long time relationships at Goldman and two Scandinavian banks had called Taylor and told him to keep Cuz away from them. They said Cuz was strident, unreasonable—too difficult to deal with. Then, on the occasional phone call between the cousins, there had been long pregnant silences. Little Cuz had wanted to tell him, and Taylor missed every nonverbal cue.

Little Cuz was foundering. He had started out following directions, and all was well. Then when Taylor went far away, it was just Cuz, all by his lonesome. This change is significant. Alchemical. Taylor's money went from active capital and business (Hunter $) to passive investments (Hearth $). In a very real way, Little Cuz morphed into his cousin's money manager! He became captain. Leader. Unfortunately, he also began to believe his own thoughts and make up his own strategies. There were no checks and balances. Little Cuz just wasn't cut out to be this kind of investment manager. The results were not pretty. The vessel took on water and emotions roiled and he panicked, and by the end of 2002 he had sunk the ship and cost Taylor what should be considered a large sum—three million dollars. He also left a hefty tax bill.

Familial and financial, the destruction was comprehensive. Little Cuz, in a sad moment of pride, dismissed the whole thing as: "Hey, I was trying my best; it's a game of risk and that's what happens sometimes. So you're out a few mill and owe the IRS a couple bucks. You scored big exercising those stock options anyway." Taylor did not take this well. The cousins, who forever had been close, had a parting of the ways and haven't really hung since.

COMMENTARY ON HUNTER $ VS. HEARTH $

There are so many black silken threads to this story. We might rightly ponder the treacherous terrain of money and family: Do we do business with those we know and love, and risk total destruction if those dealings are mishandled and fail? Or do we do business with strangers or folks with whom we have a few degrees of separation, and thereby risk loss from unexpected quarters? These are fair questions, for which there is no simple universal answer, although *Zen Money Blues* asserts that knowing your personal financial identity—your strengths and weaknesses, and how best to manage them—is the strongest ally of all. But more on that soon.

In the story of Taylor, our Elephant Hunter, the moment he stopped consistently being active in his hedge fund, that money was no longer in the domain of Hunter Money. It was Hearth Money, and finances and psyche acted accordingly. Unfortunately, Taylor was on autopilot. He did not understand the Hunter/ Hearth Money distinction, nor was he familiar with the brilliance and the blindspots of his particular ZM Type. To establish a clear vision or plan for working with an investment manager around his family money—this never dawned on him. He acted out the shadow-side of his ZM Type. The regrettable result speaks for itself.

Not long after this, Hearth Money in its undifferentiated form plagued Taylor again. The stakes were smaller this time, a passive investment in a partnership. Passive here is the operative word. He was not actively running this business. Still and all, it is shocking to note that such a successful business guy failed to do proper (really, any) due diligence on the people and the investment. He anted up on the word of a friend of a friend. Now, Taylor is a very bright guy. Yet here he was, repeating history. The wounds of his hedge fund debacle had barely begun to heal. This was no case of amnesia. Clearly, our Elephant Hunter was unable to make sense of the first wreckage.

This time, however, when the investment was foundering, he tuned in just in time to hire a good attorney and convert his debt to equity and take the helm of the company. Yes, he was able to turn it around. Of course he could. His entrepreneurial m.o. is shiny and conquering, like a great warrior in his armor. And this investment—for all intents and purposes—was now moved back to the Hunter Money domain. Not long after this episode, as we were fleshing out some of these ideas of Hunter $ vs. Hearth $, Taylor reflected: "I can always make more money. It's intense and at times all-consuming but I can always make more money. I'm not sorry I fired George and Justin and Pete; they were slacking. But I am sorry I brought out the worst in my Little Cousin. He was always very dear to me. It's not clear that our relationship will ever be right again."

Chapter 6 **The Last Word on the Hearth vs. Hunter Money Distinction**

ODAY, AS I WAS leaving the office, the phone rang. On the other end of the line was a couple—Paul and Fiona—who had been referred to me by a family therapist in Denver. The couple was at a self-identified crossroads. Retirement was anywhere from 3 to 12 years away. *That's a mighty span!* I noted. Indeed, they weren't kidding. The variables of their financial world were volatile, vertiginous, and put them on edge with each other. Precarious was a word Fiona used several times. Peter spoke of his apparent recovery from cancer, and how that intruded on his ability to "think straight" about their vision of the future. In the conversation, I myself went for the earthy comfort of the basics: *Do you know your numbers, what you have, what you owe? How have you managed and tracked things thus far? How old are you, your children? What kind of work do you do?*

On this last question Paul paused, then bared his badge of shame: *I know we should be doing better, on every front. As for my work, I am a fully tenured accounting professor at the best business school in Colorado! My word! I'm such a hypocrite!*

The poor guy was mortified. He then declared one justification after the other. None of it held sway, and he said as much. Finally the awkwardness and self-flagellation abated. Paul wanted to know what I thought. The situation was delicate. On the other hand, the truth of the dual nature of money was the best medicine. So, you can imagine how I did respond. Told him chapter and verse about making the mission-critical Hearth/Hunter Money distinction, of course.

THE
ZM TYPES:
WIRING IS WIRING

Chapter 7 ZM Types and Typology

THERE ARE PLENTY OF wonderful books out there on how to be a masterful hunter. *Zen Money Blues* is glad of that, and won't be going there. Our concern is in the other half of the picture, the half that is overlooked, the half that follows us home and—equal opportunity—can vex the B-school professor, the insurance agent, the accountant, the teacher, the actor, the financial advisor, the minister, the entrepreneur, the bureaucrat. Welcome, indeed, to the land of the Zen Money Types. It is not a moral land. It is not a land of judgment. Regardless of which ZM Type we are, each has its strengths and its weaknesses, its brilliance and its blindspots. Becoming the poster-child for personal finance (aka The Archer ZM Type) is really not the point, I assure you. There's no mold to fit into. There's no winner. That poster-child has a shadow side just like the other three ZM Types, and that shadow side is best not left unchecked. In the end, changing into one Type or another is not possible anyway. The Zen Money Types are fixed. We are who we are. We might be the great hunter who, in the village, is relegated to chores as far away as possible from managing the village's wealth; or we may find ourselves in the thick of it, handling the communal purse.

ZM: WHAT IT AIN'T

Electric blues-rock legends, Led Zeppelin, have a ripping song called "No Quarter" and, fittingly, in the chorus they sing, *They hold no quarter, they ask no quarter...* If it's been a while, it is advisable to put the album *(Houses of the Holy)* on the turntable and give that song a listen. It's all right to turn the volume all the way up. This is one of rock's enduring sounds, the bluesy spooky Robert Plant vocals mixed in with the thick resonant guitar of Jimmy Paige. However, for the pedagogical purposes of *Zen Money Blues*, kindly change the lyrics, substituting the word JUDGMENT for the word QUARTER, so that there is no misinterpretation. In ZM Typology, *They hold no judgment, they ask no judgment...*

Say "Type" and folks think, *Which Type is best? Which is worst? Which is coolest?* Folks think, *Intelligence. Judgment day. Ticket to success or failure.* Hovering is the flashback from seventh grade, the one in which you get herded into buzzing fluorescent-lit rooms for three days and fill in countless circles with a #2 pencil, and weeks later receive a number (your IQ) that is supposed to mean something about your prospects for success in the grand pecking order. Ironically, you and I both know a genius or two from those days who aced every bloody test, but was woefully lacking in common sense. Even then, you knew that "intelligence" was hardly the equivalent of enlightenment. ZM thus eschews any association with "money intelligence." It just ain't that!

There are differences in the land of ZM. Archetypal differences. Each Type has its form and function, its time and its place, its brilliance and its blindspots. This is worth keeping in mind. The Archer Type, for example, may be the poster-child for personal finance, but it is The Creative Type who can counterbalance the calculating Archer with a timely "non-money" perspective: *Honey, please. It's only money. Let's have dinner at French Laundry before we're old, wizened, and wearing dentures!* Too, The Maven Type may be exactly the guy you want to huddle with, the next time you have a budget and are planning a trip to Scottsdale, San Diego or San Francisco; but his Maven magic may be misguided, landing you in the doghouse because Scottsdale in the summer is not restful, nor is sharing a hotel port of entry with hookers in the Tenderloin. The ZM map tells many stories like this. Each Type has its mature and its undeveloped expressions. Somewhere in here that mythic village looms. Personal money has its social elements. The individual, fierce and heroic as he is, is nonetheless currently overrated. The task is bigger than that. In the end, individual intelligence is no salvation.

Which segues to an irresistible sidebar. The correlation between IQ and handling your personal money is not positive. A May 2007 article from Ohio State research scientist, Dr. Jay Zagorsky, examines the intelligence of individuals and how that affects both their personal financial management (Hearth $) and their income (Hunter $). Intelligence—and its corresponding education— is king when it comes to income. This makes sense. According to a report on the study at *http://researchnews.osu.edu/archive/ intlwlth.htm,* "the average income difference between a person with an IQ score in the normal range (100) and someone in the top 2 percent of society (130) is currently between $6,000 and $18,500 a year. But when it came to total wealth and the likelihood of financial difficulties, people of below average and average intelligence did just fine when compared with the super-intelligent."

Pondering these facts, Zagorsky poses this juicy question: *How could high-IQ people, on average, earn higher incomes but still not have more wealth than others?* Hmmm! Zagorsky has no answer for the question yet, but you can bet *Zen Money Blues* has a thing or two to say on the matter. Something funny seems to be going on in the purse of those smart earners. Something's just not matching up, like an outfit of plaid and polka-dots, like BB King singing punk rock, like smart earners suffering from a case of mistaken financial identity.

ZM Type: What It Is

ZM Type is identity. It is your ID card. That ID clarifies the rules of the personal finance game for you. It tells you not how smart you are, but rather where you are on the personal money map. You can plan; you cannot plan. You can implement; you cannot implement. You can do both; you can do neither. Everything wheels off of that ID. Who you are then expands out, defining the rules of your relationship with advisor, accountant, lawyer, and of course spouse or family members. Each Type has its own particulars. While some folks may benefit the situation by taking a chill pill, like Broccoli Raab, others will do well to empower and educate and activate themselves, like Mrs. Broccoli Raab.

ZM Typology is gleaned from answering the two truly fundamental questions of personal finance:

Are you a planner?
Are you an implementer?

This yields four possible outcomes:
yes (planner) & no (implementer) = The Architect
no (planner) & yes (implementer) = The Maven
no (planner) & no (implementer) = The Creative
yes (planner) & yes (implementer) = The Archer

Remember the recently revised Led Zeppelin riff? You know, "No Judgment." Excellent. Because there's no need to immediately adorn yourself in the safety of The Archer Type label. Yes, in the conventional view she is the poster-child for personal finance, but no, in our view, she is not the winner of the personal finance game. She is but one of the four ZM Types. As in a good epic, all the characters and all the energies and all the types have a part to play. Soon enough, you'll get acquainted with the potential enlightenment and potential blindspot of each ZM Type, and how to manage accordingly.

First let's motor back to The Inner Highway 61. On the horizon looms a small complication that can have large implications. It has to do with self-perception. For, the answer to these planner/ implementer questions should be self-evident, right? I mean, the self (who I am) and my actions (what I do) are closest to me. Wherever I go, there I am! And yet, bewildering as it is, I also recognize disconnects between who I think I am and what my actions actually are. Blindspots! Broccoli Raab thinks he is The Man in relation to money when, in reality, he is a smart earner with something funny (or not so funny) going on in his home money picture. Plaid and polka-dots.

Who Broc thinks he is flies in the face of his long-standing personal money history—history of his **actions** (erratic), history of his **emotions** (volatile), and history of his **effectiveness** (weak). Each piece figures in. Two out of three will not do. The miserable millionaire, who was effective and consistent with his actions, but feels bitter and parsimonious in the late afternoon of his life, is not someone to emulate. Life may be hard, but it's not wicked. Having a little less, with a little help from the right folks, is a palatable alternative. Enough can be enough AND mean success! In Chapter 12, this trinity of measures is revisited, accompanied by The ZM Type Quiz, to help you identify your ZM Type.

Too many folks struggle with a case of mistaken financial identity. They are not who they think they are! Financial professionals—even if they cannot name it—nonetheless recognize this phenomenon in a trice. It is the proverbial elephant in the room. The "rules of the relationship" further complicate, because therapeutic confrontation or the like is just not what financial professionals do.

In the time before the lexicon and paradigm of *Zen Money Blues*, I could not say to Broc: *Now look here, dude—tell us where you'd like to go, when you'd like to arrive, what "living the life" means to you, what experiences you can and cannot live without, and so on. Your aspirations and requirements will be taken to heart by us—your team—and added into the family financial plan. Now it is time for you to take one big step back. Have confidence in Mrs. Broc, the accountant, the bookkeeper, and me (financial advisor). Quality surrounds you, and that is good. What's more, you need your people, which is not a big deal. It just is. Like a limousine, this vehicle is not for you to drive. No freewheeling in isolation. You're The Creative Type. Your planning tends to be incomplete and your implementation tends to be inconsistent, and you are temperamental about your personal money. Therefore, you need process, rules, structure, and people. Money is best a social experience for you. Which reminds me: we'll periodically have a meeting of the minds with you. But in between meetings, please do take your chill pills.* Had I spoken this way, there'd have been no basis for it. I'd have sounded crazy. However, this is exactly what needed to be addressed, before all else. But let's let this lie for the moment, and tend to other matters, as in "growing downward." It's the roots thing! Blues are the roots for rock 'n' roll. Planning and implementing are the roots of ZM Typology. Now let's go a little deeper.

Definitions

PLAN: (noun) a detailed proposal for doing or achieving something; (verb) to decide on and arrange in advance; to design or make a plan of (something to be made or built). According to Webster's Dictionary,[2] the verb TO PLAN possesses three main senses: to ORGANIZE, to INTEND, and to DESIGN. Additionally, the word comes from the late 17th century French *plant,* as in "ground plan."

The Planner is wired accordingly: to account for and organize the myriad details of her world, which become "the design," "the picture," "the visualization." She sees the plan in her mind's eye, and does this naturally, without need of external prompting.

IMPLEMENT: (noun) a tool, utensil, or other piece of equipment, esp. as used for a particular purpose; (verb) to execute, apply, put into effect, put into action, put into practice; to fulfill, accomplish, bring about, achieve. To IMPLEMENT is rooted in the Latin verb *implere* "to fill up," and has a late Latin meaning of "to fulfill; to bring to fulfillment."

The Implementer is wired accordingly: to serve the Vision set forth by The Planner, to bring it into being, to bring it to completion, by dexterously using his many tools of "Mavenness" (about which we will learn more).

Whereas one could say The Planner displays personal financial wisdom and clarity, The Implementer exhibits skill and skillful methods. These are ideals. The former is best vision; the latter is best action. I've also been talking about ZM as "wiring." This connotes fixed elements of the money personality. You won't be changing them, any more than you will change an introvert into an extravert, or a feeling into a thinking type. That being said, Carl Jung cautions against one-sidedness of the personality. Thinking types, for example, are encouraged to develop their feeling function. In *Zen Money Blues*, the ZM Typology works a little differently.

The issue is not automatically to compensate or improve, i.e., suddenly exert to be better at balancing your checkbook, better at reading your investment statements, or better at taking the time to envision your world. The issue is one of seeing clearly your ZM Type, and managing that impeccably. You understand the qualities of your Type, the inherent strengths and weaknesses, and organize your world accordingly. Each Type has its own rules. Those rules may prescribe "you never ever try to balance a checkbook again," or that, indeed, "you need to activate yourself and assiduously balance ye olde checkbook." You may not be able to change your Type, but—in the *Zen Money Blues* universe—how you manage your ZM Type determines the outcome of the personal money game. Manage it effectively, regardless of your Type, and you generate the peace and prosperity that come from harmonizing with your money Self. This is the potent path of least resistance.

The ZM Matrix:

WHO YOU ARE WITH YOUR HEARTH MONEY

	Plan	Implement
The Architect (Celeste and Terra)	Yes	No
The Maven (New York)	No	Yes
The Creative (Thelonius Rockefeller)	No	No
The Archer (Diana)	Yes	Yes

Chapter 8

ZM Type One:

THE ARCHITECT

The Architect is the consummate planner. Design is what she sees in her mind's eye. Let's briefly recall her nature:

> The Planner is wired to account for and organize the myriad details of her world, which become "the design," "the picture," "the visualization."

ARCHITECT: PLANNER OF HEAVEN, PLANNER OF EARTH

In *Zen Money Blues*, there is one ZM Type with two distinct planner expressions, and that is The Architect. It's as if they are fraternal twins: one Celestial (Celeste) and one Earthy (Terra). They don't look alike, their values often diverge, but their "DNA" is a match. Each lays claim to being The Architect, and legitimately so. In life, planners plan to different ends, based on varied agendas and values. The results are reflected in the houses they own, the cars they drive, the outfits they don, the social status or security they achieve. Celeste and Terra are two distilled conspicuous expressions of who planners are and what they care about and how they appear to many of us. Of course, they are concepts. Most real life planner Types (The Architect) will have elements of both heaven and earth, with one element dominant. So do not let appearances deceive. You as the planner person will invariably have your own unique display of The Architect. What matters is what's inside. Wiring is wiring. Each elemental expression, and all the combinations in between, have this in common: the template of their "planner's mind" works in fundamentally the same way.

CELESTE—THE CELESTIAL ARCHITECT

First meet Celeste. She has grand designs. This never stops. Throwing a party is not just throwing a party. It is an occasion around which many will gather. There is a natural sense of celebration and relaxation and good cheer. Meticulously the menu is planned and the venue arranged. Celeste's will be among the most rockin' fêtes of the year and everyone knows it. Anticipates it. Tasty food and glorious wine flowing and guests looking super spiff. You could say there is a bit of Gatsby and Cole Porter and "Ain't Life Grand" in her!

On a more basic level, Celeste has an incredible eye for things of beauty and richness, infusing life with sparkle and style and flow. Manifesting the fruits of wealth and success are important to her. After all, success begets success. She knows this better than anyone. Even if she has not yet acquired the wealth that she desires, she has a clear picture of what she wants and how she'll put her personal money to work when she does get it. Residing in her mind are clear pictures of where she is going. She's the kind of person who lives in a very pleasant 3,000 square foot home on the golf course, and is thinking about the next thing. There's a parcel of land, a little bigger, on a quieter street, in better proximity to school and town, and she's thinking that once the boys hit elementary school age, plus the increasing flow of extended family visits, they'll really need closer to 4,500 square feet just to keep the peace. A thought like this is a rare event for The Creative or The Maven ZM Types. The Celestial Architect, however, doodles and sketches like this all the time. It may take her and hubby a couple of years to gather the funds, buy the land, draw up the plans, sell the current house, build the new house, and make the transition. That's OK. The plans are already there, detailed and organized, regarding their quite literal "next big move."

A more contemplative version of Celeste is also to be found, not on society's pages, not in Saks Fifth Avenue or Nordstrom, but closer to Walden Pond and Chautauquas and the Williamsburg section of Brooklyn, where the premium is on simplicity and independence. Celeste's vision is to have the fewest possible material demands made on her time and energy. She is writer, artist, intellectual, sculptor, healer, and such. She serves her Muse, first and foremost. I think of the great heroes of Black Jazz, who for generations not only kept the music alive, they kept it flowing and growing into—arguably—America's greatest cultural gift to the world. There was no great financial payoff for those artists. Just the love of their art. Just serving the Muse. The community was enriched by these artists, these vanguards of culture. Not surprisingly, the high art of jazz occupied a revered place in the community.

"Celeste of Walden Pond" is a kindred version of this phenomenon. Keeping her personal money universe lean is intentional. It is reflective of a clean, clear, thought-through plan. She might be the woman who edits your book, or the professor who teaches at your daughter's college, or the teacher at your teenager's high school: these folks sure as shootin' are not doing it for the money! They're doing it for the love. Keeping simple the design of their personal financial life is not only practical, it gives duration to what they are offering the world (Hunter activity). What all of these folks share is this: they know their priorities, and live accordingly.

Celeste of Walden Pond is an important reminder of the ethos of *Zen Money Blues*. You may recall the earlier vamp about "money and non-money." Well, this is to that point. Whereas most of us do our Hunter thing (i.e., make money) to serve our Hearth life (i.e., home, education, vacation, new duds), Celeste of Walden Pond does exactly the opposite. She does her personal finance vision thing to serve her work life—which may not pay a whole lot. Thus, the impetus for planning comes from the other side. Beauty is simplicity, and lightness of personal financial load. Beauty is not found in more things, but in service and writing and art and culture and travel and teaching and reading and nature and work-well-done. Beauty is being able to do something you love (your life's work) and not be tyrannized by money, because you keep your personal money requirements simple and clean. Economy matters, even on "the road less traveled by."[3] Probably the world could use more folks like this. Whatever the case, *Zen Money Blues* offers counsel on this point. If you want to do this, or feel that you MUST do this, then do it right! For there are a lot of folks who essay to live the artist's life or the contemplative's life or bohemian-wanderer's life or inventor's life or according to some other heaven-sent inspiration, but have no real plan for doing it. Not so, for Celeste of Walden Pond! She's thought it all through. She's gotten down to the bones of what she really needs, and all else she's left behind.

Back East where I grew up, you'll still find folks who fit the old money "waspy" stereotype. They are well off, have a nice house and the country club membership, send their kids to prep school, but they are not extravagant. In fact, they epitomize the expression "Yankee frugal." Very clear about their priorities (a critical planning virtue), they live to travel or help their kids out or serve in the not-for-profit sector. Their vision is a fascinating amalgamation of Thoreau and Cole Porter, of Walden Pond and Yale Blue. Planning-in-action goes in a variety of directions. Sometimes it is unabashedly materialistic. More often there is a strong aesthetic at play, or pristine vision of what is important and harnessing energy and resources to serve that. The results are manifold. They could be self-serving, or they could be social elixir. Could give duration to art and culture and good works and medicine. Whatever road The Architect takes, whatever metaphorical house she builds, she is well endowed with the gift of vision, organization, and intent. In the realm of personal finance, these are auspicious gifts.

TERRA—THE EARTHY ARCHITECT

Now meet Terra. Well, actually it is an unscheduled visit and she's a little busy at the moment. On her way out the door with a formidable list of appointments and to-do's, into the old Volvo station wagon, and there she goes. Bye-bye.

Time for Plan B. It looks like some *Zen Money Blues* narrative will have to do. In the land of personal money, Terra means business. She too is a planner. A most excellent planner, day-in day-out, breakfast lunch and dinner. Tea time and laundry time besides, and visit the doctor time and go to market time, and you get the drift. Feasts are pleasant enough, but each day is a production unto itself. She can lay it all out and make sense of it. It's not that she has to do it all, any more than air traffic control needs to literally get in the cockpit and land every single airplane. Rather, she organizes, directs, coordinates, and manages. That takes a planner!

Terra is predisposed to finding herself in "the millionaire next door" category, (particularly if she happens to marry a Maven or Archer ZM Type.) She doesn't need to show off the accoutrements of wealth. Is more than happy to live in the same house for 25 years or longer, owned free and clear, and drive the old car, also owned free and clear, though in this day and age, she might be seen driving the same hybrid Prius for the next 8 years. Being earthy, organized, and steadfast are her main moves. She sees what needs to be done and does it. Emphasis is on that first part: she sees what needs to be done.

Terra is the constant gardener. Ruminates on the elements and conditions that assure nourishment and growth. Nothing flashy. Makes a list, sees that it is completed. Makes another list. Sees that through, too. If Celeste is concerned with picking the low hanging fruit of life, and celebrating and displaying it, Terra is focused on the nurturance of that seed and sapling. Nurturing, be it of children or garden or personal finances, is naturally a long-term proposition. Things take time. Terra can nurture a vision that extends far into the future. This is her power.

Terra is like a good Chicago mayor. OK, maybe a bit bossy, and maybe gets into everyone's business, but she knows what needs to be done to run a city, or a family: lots of details, lots of projects, lots of plans. She is the practical Architect Type. She knows what it takes to pull off dinner, the birthday party, or the school play; and she knows when it's time to go to Bloomingdale's to buy new "bloomies," procure new leggings, socks, ties, ascots, handkerchiefs, and so on; she's always thinking, that Terra, and it never tires her out. She knows that it won't all get done today and that tomorrow's another day, and she'll be ready for that too, list in hand!

Identifying the myriad lifestyle wants and needs of your self and your family is easier said than done. Terra gathers the heap and sorts through the details and makes sense of things: clothes for biz, fun, working out; food for health and the army of adolescents ransacking the fridge; home that lays out right—to chill, entertain, or work in. Logistics are her forte. Terra's feet are on the ground. Her plans include planning for the unexpected. Life insurance, good medical insurance, long-term care; all make her feel secure, and she wants to know the scoop on them. In the financial planning business, Terra is a voracious student of the game. She is not freaked out about planning for disability or death, just because it's a beautiful day and those are macabre matters. She's running her city: the subways and the water works and sanitation need to be tended to!

Like no other, save The Archer, Terra can think long-term. Wants to gain the long-term picture. In the investment management world, there is an oft-used expression: "growing oak trees." Folks who embrace this are way ahead in the game. Are bound to get on famously with experienced investment advisors. The Terra Architect Type gets it immediately. She knows in her bones that "growing oak trees" is such a solid way to invest. It's the most basic wisdom of the earth, the cycles of nature. Things take time. Restlessness is ill-advised. Simplicity is actually quite sophisticated. Those who see this and feel this possess uncommon common sense. They display prudence; hence they make no bad mistakes. In the engineering parlance, you could say there is no design flaw. This is a beautiful thing. Terra keeps it real. Chipping away at saving for retirement, squirreling away funds for the children's education, planning for life's inevitable difficult climes—this is Terra's patient, methodical approach, and there is great strength and stability in this.

Non-planner ZM Types (Creative, Maven) go shopping at Nordstrom, and come home with new clothes yet no new outfits. Non-planners go shopping at Whole Foods, and come home with bags of groceries yet no menu of meals. The fridge has yogurt and potatoes and celery and milk and butter, and the cupboards have pasta and rice and breakfast cereal and salad dressing; and dinner ends up being peanut butter on bananas. Sounds like the stereotypical bachelor pad of yesteryear, where potatoes with butter and yogurt and anything else in the fridge was the go-to meal. I mention these examples, not just to reminisce on how uncivilized life can be without the earthy and heavenly designs of The Architect, but to straightforwardly address The Common Sense Question:

Do people really not know what they need or want? Actually, The Common Sense Question requires sharpening:

> Do people really not know what they need and want
> in time, while they can still do something about it?

Strangely, experience and observation show that a slew of folks need some sort of external prompting. Someone to ignite the thought process and the conversation, be it spouse, thought-partner, adult child, or financial professional. Once the engine is started, people know where to go and what the destination looks like. In the absence of that external prompting, non-planner Types (Creative, Maven) naturally employ their own autopilot mode. Why? Simply put, wiring is wiring. Non-planner people don't think to plan. Not until they are asked to think about it.

And again, by planning I mean good planning, comprehensive planning. Thus the answer is this: NO—many people really don't know what they want or need in time to do something about it, unless they are prompted from without!

The Architect ZM Type herself needs no activation, no external prompting. Naturally she sees planning in vivid pictures and copious lists, and lives life through the splendor of the senses. Retirement for her is not a number (*We have two million dollars in stocks and bonds; we're golden!*). The Architect sees retirement as good living: robust activities, worldly people, sparkling landscapes, artful entrées, and a menu of savory choices. Or sees peace and quiet amid refined company and pastoral settings. Or sees security and comfort: hosting the grandchildren, drinking iced tea and visiting with long-time neighbors, doing small projects on that house in the country, and excursions to Little Italy or Big Italy. Saving for college for her children is not a dutiful abstraction: she sees her progeny in college—just as she herself once was!

The Architect ZM Type is wired to plan. To organize, to intend, to design. The countenance of The Architect can vary greatly. But whatever her appearance, whatever her values, the truth of her financial identity can't be diluted. She is The Architect. The template of her activity is fundamentally consistent. Wiring is wiring. The Architect knows how to plan comprehensively, already plans comprehensively, and these characteristics differentiate her from The Creative and The Maven Types. However, there are three not-so-small areas (also known as "blindspots") that The Architect will have to reckon with. These are the Three P's: Prioritizing, Price, and Planner-itis.

Blindspots for The Architect ZM Type

Prioritizing and Puella

Each ZM Type has its brilliance and its blindspots. Thus it is for The Architect. Autopilot, you may recognize by now, refers to that undeveloped, unreflecting mode of operating that, in the Hearth Money realm, can be problematic. Maturity is often lacking. Carl Jung, in his psychological writings, used the terms "puer" and "puella"—describing personalities who cling to a youthful state of innocence. In mythology, the puella is a child-god. In everyday life, the puella (literally "girl" in Latin) is someone who doesn't want to grow up in certain ways. The decisions of the adult world are depressing. In personal finance, this puer/puella phenomenon can be the shadow of the The Architect ZM Type. *I want it all. So leave me alone. I don't want to deal with choosing some things and cutting out others.* For The Architect, messing with the picture is, um, not welcome! *The picture is crystal clear, complete; can't you see that? You want another picture? You want people in my neighborhood, in my city, to starve?*

Naturally, The Architect does the "blue sky" thing. She visualizes unfettered her world and all the elements therein. This visualization is detailed and thorough and all-inclusive. Next comes a task. She is to give her vision gravitas. The sky is blue, but choices must be made. The task is to focus, prioritize, channel resources in a select few directions.

The Architect is wired to prioritize, in fact. There is no deficiency here. Indeed, in the managing-your-ZM Type section of this book ("Money Mandala Rx"), there is considerable discourse on why it is ill-advised that The Architect neglect this gift with its accompanying responsibility. She is born with an excellent discriminating sword. A sword that cuts through and prioritizes, and budgets.

Cutting through takes exertion, maturity, detachment, and commitment. Like no other, she can discern and decide and arrange and design the elements accordingly.

But will she?

Prioritizing is polite for budgeting. Not sexy, for sure. In fact, to the immature (puella) Architect, it's a drag. Really, best forgotten! Celeste wants what she wants. That beautiful object here now: *It's a one of a kind piece—personal art!* Terra herself becomes a bit of a freight train about budget and priorities: *What do you mean less pasture-raised organic beef from Whole Foods? How do you DO LESS—starve the troops?! Oh, cut back on the clothing purchases; fine, go to work naked—you'll look better anyway, particularly with the weight you're about to lose eating rice and beans. My word!*

You can't live without The Architect's enriching "planning" wisdom, or her irrepressible *joie de vivre,* though you'd better watch out, because unchecked, she knows how to spend money! The puella/puer aspect exponentially raises the stakes. Making more money won't solve the problem: The Architect ZM Type has already got plans for that too! Indeed, you've got a real live one on your hands, unless and until she accepts the responsibility and the burden of wielding that sharp sword, and cuts, and prioritizes.

PRICE AND DICE

Price is in the blindspot, as well. The Architect doesn't want to be hassled by it. *Already there is so much to be done! Who's got time for this? Does it really matter? Do we have to care about price all the time—how dreary!* Or, variation on that theme, she simply doesn't look at price! What she puts on the charge card does not especially register in her mind. Until it catches up with her. And it will catch up with her. Middle class, rich middle class, humble mega-wealthy, moderately mega-wealthy: it will catch up with The Architect. Except for God and billionaires, personal financial resources are finite. That's a part of the ground rules. Thrift does matter. Prioritizing does matter. Skillful dealings do matter. How the plan gets implemented can be the critical difference between success and failure.

Deciding to care and be better at price isn't going to work either. Celeste and Terra's heart is not in it. Rarely will you see them haggling for the deal, or if they do, it'll be pretty weak. At implementation time, The Architect is no match for The Maven ZM Type. There is special knowledge and skill, plus a certain love for the deal, that The Architect will never possess. Celeste sees beauty and goes straight to it—no sale rack or buying the nearly new car with 4,000 miles on it. Terra's going straight to Whole Foods and doing the whole shop then and there: who cares if Whole Foods is 15% more expensive than Trader Joe's? Who has time to shop in two stores, or buy bulk and figure out unit costs per item? Not Terra.

Regarding price, there's another rather sensitive matter. The Architect just doesn't know price, even if she tries. Her thoughts about price have a tendency to be unhelpful. More precisely, the word is "erratic." The Architect has erratic price thoughts. As you will see in Money Mandala Rx, The Architect is well served to take note of prices but not derive meaning or conclusions from them, especially regarding major purchases and investments. Price is simply information that she best processes with her Maven Type spouse/friends or professional advisors, or compares that information with what she reads in Consumer Reports (if she reads Consumer Reports!). Price, however, is not something that she will know with any real consistency: it's a roll of the dice for The Architect. Of course, if she loves golf and really makes a consistent eBay study of golf club merchandise, she will probably do all right. Still, she might miss a key detail that Mavens would know, such as the fact that there has been a recent epidemic of counterfeit name-brand clubs sold over the internet and now she might own a set of them! This is case in point of The Architect trying to do good by price, but meeting with mixed results.

Even Celeste of Walden Pond—she'd be power-frugal if she could, but she can't. Left to her own devices, she will miss the mark. She needs others, namely Mavens. It is true that, by definition, there's no puella in her personal money self, because Celeste of Walden Pond prioritizes and cuts and keeps things as simple as she can. But that discipline won't help her when it comes time to implement. Be it shopping, investing, purchasing the cabin by the pond, buying used books or a Vermont Castings® wood stove. Here self-reliance will not do. She'll leave too much money on the table. She'll leave too much meat on the bone. Planning she can do in spades. Implementation, as it is for The Architect ZM Type as a whole, is best a social experience for her.

PLANNER-ITIS AND INVESTMENTS

Planner-itis is a comical phenomenon, just as long it's not you that's a part of it. Then it gets on your nerves. It works like this. You have a plan. It's a good plan. Plans, of course, are never perfect. The direction should be right, but the human condition says this: there will be obstacles. The best of plans meets with unforeseen bumps in the road. Just because this occurs does not mean your plan is bunk. But that's what planner-itis is: the habit of ditching the current plan as soon as it meets with obstacles and making a new plan in its stead. Talk about self-sabotage. Ouch!

Naturally, some plans are flawed, or need to be adjusted to include new information or changing conditions. This is true with investments. But there's a world of difference between tweaking a plan and going back to the drawing board. Sticking with an imperfect plan is generally much, much better than the habitual 86'ing of plans. The critical question is this: Is your plan good enough? The good-enough plan is often a very good plan, albeit with a few of life's bumps and bruises on it. Of course, if you have a truly bad plan, cut your losses and move on. However, if you have too many "bad plans" in your wake, then either someone is not very good at planning or you have a very real case of planner-itis.

Investors do some nutty things with their investment dollars, and planner-itis is one of them. Ditching a perfectly good investment plan, because it is biased to value stocks and it is a "growth stocks market," for example, is an unpropitious practice. Same goes for ditching a growth portfolio in a period when value stocks are outperforming. Or, like too many did in the late 90's, deciding that diversification is for the birds and selling all their bonds. Or, as one investor told me after he'd had two years of "success" with mortgage REITS: "they can replace bonds in the portfolio, because they deliver much better returns and are just as safe as bonds." If only! The list goes on. All reflect a certain lack of investment discipline.

I was tempted to say "simple" lack of discipline, but that would not be true: discipline in investing is far from simple. Might be the hardest thing of all. That would be my vote. Nonetheless, knowing and doing are not the same. Just ask Terra, who absolutely knows the merits of long-term investing. She's on board. But that knowledge doesn't translate into her doing the plan, and doing it well. Why this is so, is a bit of a mystery. With The Creative ZM Type, it's easy to see why he bails on investment plans: he's emotional! Emotions and investing are not an ideal combo. Already, The Creative Type is inclined to buy high when he feels optimistic and sell low when he feels scared. With The Architect, however, the dynamics are not so overt. I've seen some Architects seduced by greed and restlessness, and hence chase returns. I've seen many implement without passion and discernment, receive middling returns, and conclude the problem must be the plan. I've seen others flat-out neglect to follow through on implementing their investment plan. Or set it up and then stop working it, many times due to unforeseen commitments, waning interest, or no reason to speak of. But beyond reason or no reason, beyond tricky emotions or sudden bright ideas, the implementation of the investment plan isn't as strong and steady as it deserves to be. As it needs to be.

Successful investing is about doing the little things well. Picking a money market fund for your brokerage account should be easy. But pay attention you must, or risk finding yourself in a fund backed by sub-prime investments that expose your principal to loss. Yes, money markets can have loss of principal. The Maven knows this. The Archer knows this. It's all in the prospectus. Tax efficient investment vehicles and low internal expenses—these are the little things that position one for success, or, when overlooked, position one for the long fall to mediocrity. Changing to a "new, better" plan won't get it done. It's beside the point. All the while, The Architect's goals hang precariously in the balance.

. . . .

EXEUNT CELESTE AND TERRA

In the gospel of *Zen Money Blues*, The Architect's job is divine—to design and organize all of heaven and earth. In this she is active. In this she takes the lead, thank God. But implementing that plan is another matter altogether. Implementation requires different chops. Different personal money DNA—different as night and day, sun and moon, queen and duke. Here opposites complement each other, rather than conflict or detract. The Maven ZM Type, at his brilliant best, is that complementary opposite. He is the perfect knight for The Architect. Perfect insofar as he stabilizes and supports and protects and actualizes The Architect's vision— if she will be humble at the right time (the time of implementation) and follow The Maven's jaunty lead.

PITH SUMMARY OF THE ARCHITECT ZM TYPE
PLANNER: YES. IMPLEMENTER: NO.

Chapter 9

ZM Type Two:

THE MAVEN

NICKNAMES: THE MARKET MAKER, NEW YORK
PLANNER: NO. IMPLEMENTER: YES.

The Maven is the quintessential implementer. Taking action is what he naturally does. Let's remember his calling:

> The Implementer is wired to serve the Vision set forth by The Planner, to bring it into being, to bring it to completion, by dexterously using his many tools of "Maven-ness."

MAVEN

The Maven is the implementer extraordinaire. The word "Maven" has the connotation of connoisseur. Where to stay when in San Francisco, New York, Paris: ask The Maven. Buying a car: he tells you that the Audi dealer in Fort Collins is leasing the A6 for $125/month less than the Boulder dealer, and he'll tell you not to waste your time or money thinking about the A8. Buy glorious wine, right year, right region of the world, right price: ask The

Maven. Where to vacation—Costa Rica, Nicaragua, Mexico, Maui—when, and how best to get in and out, which airlines—and whether you should consider buying land or a timeshare or a house down there: yes, consult The Maven. Obviously, no one Maven fits all. If you are lucky, you can rely on several of them, depending on what is to be implemented. Mavens naturally love a deal.

"Market Maker" is the more inclusive moniker of this Maven ZM Type. The Market Maker displays Maven-ness about not only the elegant and the refined, but the bawdy and the commonplace. For example, you probably would not call someone a connoisseur of toilet paper, nor would you call up a Maven for where to get the best deal on toilet paper. But if there were a great deal on Charmin® at Costco, the Market Maker would be coming home with an extra package of it. He'd look at it on the shelf and go: *Hmmm, now that's a good price for that!*—and down comes another 16-roll package of Charmin into his shopping cart. It is his ability to know the market—even mundane markets—and his interest in registering the myriad details of price and brand, that make him such a superior implementer. He knows who is selling what where, at what price, perhaps to whom, and how often. He knows the details like a Wall Street specialist, as if he were making markets so that others could buy and sell. He might not do it consciously. Either way, one thing is for sure: there's a lot of strong reliable data that goes into the statement: *Hmmm, now that's a good price for that!*

Of course, when the Market Maker comes home with an extra package of Charmin and the whole family is morbidly constipated and it's All-Bran® they need, you might agree that while the Market Maker is a hell of an implementer, he is underwhelming in the area of planning. The Market Maker is not thinking about the grand scheme of things. He does not have the planner mojo thing. He is master of the present moment. He is master of the transaction. We call him "New York" because he is tough and smart and has a tremendous sense of humor and gamesmanship. We also call him New York because sometimes he thinks he is the center of the universe, which arguably he is, but he gets caught up in this and forgets about the rest of the world; namely, that not every social interaction is about the deal. I mean, when you want to make love to your lover, you don't really want to cut corners on flowers, dinner, or getting in the mood, right?

Yard Sailors (or so they are named 'round here) are a breed unto themselves, and definitely Mavens. Bright and curly every Saturday morning they sail through urban and suburban neighborhoods, in search of yard sales. Good yard sales with good stuff, which means getting there before other Sailors get there. Sailors love the game of making markets, of analyzing the worth of the seller's wares, even if they're *tchotchkes,* which they usually are! An added bonus is playing detective/psychologist, sizing up the seller (often a Maven himself!) and surmising what his half-disclosed motivations for selling his schtuff might be. Which leads into negotiation. The art of the deal! The Sailor gets it started: *That old holey sock is worth 20 bucks and not a penny more!* On this fine spring morning, the seller is no slouch himself and rebuts: *Can't do it. I paid 40 bucks for that holey sock, back in the day, late sixties Haight Ashbury. It can only have appreciated these many years. But the time has come for me and it to part ways. 35 bucks and not a penny less!* And away they go. In the end, on a good day, the Yard Sailor will get the full-contact encounter he energetically seeks. The tussle, the haggle, the matching of market wits. Without it, he might still gain the trinket for a song, but feel less than fulfilled.

MAVEN-AS-IMPLEMENTER: MASTER OF FRUGAL CHIC

The Maven is indispensable in The Architect's personal financial universe. Once Celeste or Terra gives him the list, or seeks his advice, he is a tremendous resource. The Maven loves to help. He is proud of his special knowledge and skill, and typically very happy to share. How to proceed then is simple: follow his instruction. Malcolm Gladwell, in his bestseller, *The Tipping Point*, waxes on about The Maven Type, and introduces the reader to an energetic, successful economist from the University of Texas who disdained paying retail for staying at the five-star hotels; and to display his prowess, he tells Gladwell whom to call at The Park Central Hotel in Manhattan and how to inquire, to get the insider's rate. It doesn't matter how wealthy The Maven is; he knows the value of a nickel and never forgets that.

So before acquiring things, or acquiring experiences, one is well served to consult The Maven and his New York cousin, The Market Maker. It is true, as we already know, The Maven can be an insufferable know-it-all, and have his own version of bossy, but if he's good, it's worth the trouble. Generally speaking, The Architect and The Creative Types should refrain from trying to act like Mavens. They should simply find one for the task at hand and solicit his advice and take action on it. It's also fine, of course, if The Maven will handle the matter altogether.

Balance the checkbook, download and track every penny on Quicken, pay the bills, and do it twice a month, month after month; this is what The Maven (the consummate implementer of the plan) is made for. He's a rock. He should be doing this. Family finances stay sane when bills are paid promptly. Handling all the sundry transactions and interactions also go to The Maven-as-implementer, be they with the plumber or car repair guy or painter or landscaping crew. There is a watchful eye to the exchange of value, and hence accountability. Build a new house or do a remodel: the general contractor ought to be an excellent implementer sort. A Maven Type will of course find the best general contractor for the job. Regarding investments, The Maven awaits the careful crafting of the plan (aka: The Investment Policy Statement), with the family's core objectives and risk tolerance imbedded in it. Then he moves into action. If the plan calls for some private real estate investments, The Maven will work the scene till he finds "best in class for the right price." If the plan calls for a broadly diversified portfolio of stocks and bonds, The Maven will carefully judge the prospects of passive vs. active management. More than anyone, The Maven understands how to generate or discover "alpha" (i.e., added value) in a portfolio. But the history of the stock market teaches humility too, for "alpha" is very hard to come by, so he'll also be considering the merits of keeping internal expenses and taxes down, both of which are typically associated with passive investment styles. While The Architect ZM Type will establish what the goals are, how much she needs and when, what kind of risk/return universe to inhabit and so on, The Maven will work the plan and work it good.

In the end, no one does frugal like The Maven! *Whole Foods doesn't own the market in organic food*, declares The Maven. *Try Trader Joe's or Vitamin Cottage or, don't look now, check out A&P and Safeway!* The Maven can even do "Frugal-Chic," which is both stylish and impressive. There is a store here in Boulder called "Rags." It's a high-end consignment store for women's clothes. Most of the items, beautiful garments acquired at the Neiman Marcuses and Saks Fifths of the world, have never been worn. How that came to be, ahem, will not be analyzed. But you can guess who regularly buzzes over there, like a bee to nectar. And don't be surprised if the parking area out front is filled with nice cars. Maven-ness is not bound by socioeconomics. Upper middle-class Mavens love a deal just as much as middle-class Mavens love a deal! They may be quirky, they may be pushy, but they sure are handy to have around when it's time to make any plan a reality.

Blindspots for The Maven ZM Type

The Raven Maven

The shadow side of The Maven (The Raven Maven) brings to mind Oscar Wilde's trenchant description of the cynic as "a man who knows the price of everything and the value of nothing."[4] The Maven-as-implementer can at times get carried away in his pursuit of the deal. He can chase price and forget quality. He can negotiate such a good deal that the other party feels manipulated—worse, feels like a commodity—and no longer wishes to wholeheartedly honor the terms set forth, thereby diminishing the exchange. Or Mavens can "think price" at exactly the wrong time. For example, Mavens can be notoriously fee sensitive, and not want to spend money on professional advice, which they then forego, and which they then regret. Everyone seems to love to hate attorneys (at least that is what one hears these days), but a good attorney with expertise and experience will save your bacon.

I am reminded of a West Coast copyright lawyer whom a client and I consulted. In the first minute of the preliminary phone call, we found out he normally required a $25,000 retainer and charged $600/hour, which made my client gasp, and rightly so, until we learned who this guy was. First his father and then he had written the book—literally—that the top law schools use for studying copyright law, not to mention composed some of the most enduring statutes. In fact, in our stated area of need, an obscure liturgical niche, he had already been in the thick of it with similar cases. This was our guy. He had answers. His authority was obvious. During the call, we inquired about the possibility of bypassing the retainer and procuring a two-hour consult, given my client's dedication to community service. Our Esteemed Esquire chuckled and said, *My friends, this won't take but 30 minutes!* Suddenly we had such a deal, and authoritative answers, from a veritable institution of the copyright law universe. And sure enough, the meeting with the attorney went according to script, the client getting the goods in fewer than 30 minutes. Now, stepping back for a moment, it is fair to assert that the price myopic Raven Maven would have aborted this mission after the first minute of the phone call. *$600 bucks an hour! What are you nuts?* But that would have been costly. Would have separated him from the very thing that makes him special: best information.

As noted heretofore, The Maven doesn't do planning. If he has a list in his hands, it's a safe bet that he did not write it. Not the first time, anyway. If he comes home from Nordstrom and in fact has some outfits that work, it is a safe bet that he let a salesperson help him. This is no overt diss. He is who he is. Wiring is wiring. To counterbalance The Maven's no-show on the planning side, he unequivocally needs relationship, and it is relationship that The Raven Maven repels. The Maven wants a deal, even on services provided by others. The Maven doesn't want to pay full price, might even want to dictate to the professional how it should go. *No offense, Counselor, but this contextual data-gathering, relationship-building thing is unnecessary. I don't need to pay you to get to know me, my background, my successes and failures, or my overall values and objectives. Just give me the information I need. Should I sue the bastard?!*

What's more, relationships are messy. Some people deliver what they say they will, and some don't. That variation in quality delivered is vexing. Nor can it be 100% controlled, and, well, it's kind of obvious, The Maven likes control and likes his predictable outcomes. He'll bet on himself. But betting on other people doesn't feel so good. *Next time I'll pay myself the 1,000 bucks to come up with the same crappy facile advice I paid my attorney for!*

The Raven Maven definitely prefers the devil he knows (himself) to the devil he doesn't know (an expert professional or service person). Free help is OK, but the Raven Maven otherwise doesn't want to pay. Shopping price on therapists and medical specialists or legal specialists or financial planners is something The Raven Maven would like to do. Of course, the best professionals have neither interest nor need to negotiate fees with anyone, least of all someone who appears to be potentially very annoying. And this is a great loss for The Maven ZM Type, who really does need these relationships. Needs the perspective and ken and counterbalance of a good financial planner, accountant, family attorney, as well as all the other players who remove bottlenecks—bookkeepers, gardeners, mechanics, acupuncturists, and so on.

Relationship runs counter to transacting. Mavens like to transact. Carried into personal relationships, say around family and money, this aversion to relationship and obsession with transactions can be very dangerous. The Raven Maven can be intensely critical and condescending toward a non-Maven spouse. Recently I saw this acted out around the "let's build a house" ritual. I was not the only witness. The whole dang neighborhood was, for this became the construction project from hell, the one that would never go away, with heavy and light trucks blowing through and nail-guns firing at all hours and radios blaring. What was an easy six- to nine-month build took almost two years. Along the way, it must have been sheer madness. One can only imagine The Raven Maven stalking his Celestial wife's every move—from choices on doorknobs to moldings to counter tops to wood floors. As many folks know, the details on such a project are endless: every day the project must have been marred with one row after another. Their interaction was the opposite of complementary. Not that it's fair to completely blame The Raven Maven, but his is a very inflexible Type. Whatever the case, the outcome was one house, coming in way over budget, with irate neighbors who called the city several times, and, last but not least, a Celestial wife who wanted out of the marriage. Only there was a problem. They were too poor to divorce. Having funds to live a very pleasant, rich middle-class existence is not the same as having funds for two simultaneous versions of that. So he lives in a house with a woman who wants him out. That kind of miserable self-imprisonment typifies the trouble that The Raven Maven can get himself into.

. . . .

NEW YORK

The Maven's job is gritty, and at times heroic—to implement the carefully wrought personal financial plan. In this he is active. In this he takes the lead. He's New York. He is that perfect knight for The Architect. He's tenacious, and will make you laugh, make you crazy, or both. But planning in the personal financial realm is another matter altogether. And there's that not so small matter about Raven Maven-ness. Devaluing relationships. Getting caught in price myopia. For all of that, he will do well by The Architect, if he lets that relationship be complementary instead of a source of conflict. Then The Architect will elegantize The Maven. Civilize his activities. Guide his way. And ensure meaning on his quest.

But only if The Maven will be humble at the right time, and value a variety of quality relationships, and let in the bigger view of The Architect and The Creative.

PITH SUMMARY OF THE MAVEN ZM TYPE
PLANNER: NO. IMPLEMENTER: YES.

Chapter 10

ZM Type Three:
THE CREATIVE

NICKNAME: THELONIUS ROCKEFELLER
PLANNER: NO. IMPLEMENTER: NO.

Note: It is easy to picture folks identifying themselves as The Architect and saying, *Yes, I'm organized and see a variety of detailed pictures, though I'm not much for watching price or implementing like The Maven.* For The Maven, self-identification may be a tad more work. If you don't really know "planning," with its ability to know BOTH the big picture AND the thousand details, then it's hard to appreciate what you don't really know; and so The Maven might say, *Hey, I can plan: I don't see what the big deal is!* Planning is somewhat elusive in concept, though in practice it's quite straightforward. Plans, priorities, lists, organization. Either you approach your Hearth Money world this way, or you don't. You know where I'm going with this. It may take a while, even some good old-fashioned test taking, but The Maven will eventually spot himself and say: *I can Mavenize, no doubt about that. But truth be told, my planning chops are middling. I can see that now.* For The Creative Type, however, self-identification (i.e., what ZM Type am I?) is complicated. Very complicated.

To get a handle on this, let's start at the beginning, and pose this question: Who wants to (voluntarily) join the ZM club that declares: *we're not planners, we're not implementers*? Not that we sufficiently know what that "no planner/no implementer" declaration means, but it certainly appears that this is the "loser's club!" That is rather scathing, and seems good reason for self-deception.

Actually, I just put Zeppelin on the turntable again, hoping to assuage that voice of judgment. But you're not convinced. Fair enough. Still, this is worth drilling deeper into, because every one of us hears the "chorus," the super-ego voice of these modern times. Is it from the mass media? Is it from our childhood? Is it from our spouse who's fed up? Did we make it up ourselves? Whatever the case, it goes something like: *Grow up! Get your money act together! Optimize! Hello!* And in the modern world, wherein that mythic village is nowhere to be seen, you are left with no choice: you better get it together. This is life. You suck it up and make the best of it.

The consistent quality and effectiveness of your planning and implementing is another matter. You did the best you could. This was proper. Who else was going to do it, anyway? Actually, that's a very good question, to be taken up again and again, particularly in The Creative's "Money Mandala Rx" section. For now, however, let us honor the fact that you've done what had to be done. And, let's add a new level to this discourse: objectivity. It's OK now to evaluate the quality and effectiveness and consistency of your Hearth Money activities. Getting a grade of "C" in planning, in the *Zen Money Blues* view, simply means this: you're not a planner. Mediocrity does not equal failure. It just means you need to reorient. Doing more or reading more is not where the payoff is. No more uber-individualism is prescribed, where your personal finances are concerned. Objectively judging your personal money-in-action is OK. If you're Maven-ness is predominantly mediocre, that too is important information. There's no loser, for sure. Kindly be open to this objective view, especially because this might be very hard for you.

Last factor in why it is so dang difficult for you, Dear Creative Type, to see yourself, besides fear of being a loser and fear of personal financial damnation, is this: Looks can be deceiving. The Creative Type does not require that you be Bjork or Phil or moe. or Radiohead. Nor must you move through the world in exotic outfits and movie-star glasses. The financial services profession contains a preponderance of Creative Types. Bespectacled and donning conservative business suits, these bankers and money managers and financial advisors hardly fit the picture of The Creative. By day, they act as the village, the money mandala, the circle of trusted professionals for other families. This is their Hunter world, and many are quite good at what they do. Yet in the privacy of their own homes, where Hearth $ is Hearth $ and *not* Hunter $, the rules change. For some, indeed, there they are: mediocre in planning, mediocre in implementing, apropos their own family money. By day, they're objective and skillful for the client. At home, that acumen is nowhere to be seen! So, please don't be deceived by looks, or profession, or a healthy confident male ego. Don't be deceived by others. Don't deceive yourself. Wiring is wiring. No way around it. Once upon a modern time, you needed to survive in the personal finance realm; you gave it your best shot; now there's a better way. And it all begins with coming home to who you are, to your true financial identity.

Then you can create and activate your Money Mandala, your people, and that will be a genuine delight.

THE CONTROVERSIAL CREATIVE ZM TYPE

Of all four Types, The Creative is the one to be stranded on a desert island with. He is the one most likely to make lemonade out of lemons. To feel wealth as much bigger than money. To feel life as so much bigger than money. This makes him fun and lovable. At his best, he breaks the rules of personal finance at the right time. This makes him a natural born risk taker. But there is a problem. There is a very real possibility here of damnation by faint praise, unless it is qualified. In character and mien and action, not all Creatives are alike. Yes, they all share the same personal finance wiring. But, no, they don't go in the same direction. The implications of this are dramatic. As it pertains to personal money, The Awake Creative, for example, is likely to be one of the most chill, accommodating, and generous people you ever meet, while The Arrogant Creative can be one of the most charming, fun, controlling, and tyrannical. One Type, two very different characters.

But the controversy of The Creative is more basic than even light and dark. It comes of its very essence, which implacably asserts this:

> The Creative ZM Type has no business doing his personal financial planning and implementation by himself.

This is such an insult in the modern world, particularly for any of us who are well educated and of sufficient means. It's as if someone tried to take away our personal freedoms. It's an indignity of the first degree. Nonetheless, this is a Rinzai moment for *Zen Money Blues*. The assertion stands. The modern world is wrong. The uber-individual view is confused. Look at what The Architect does, look at what The Maven does:

> The Creative ZM Type will never attain such a sustained level of envisioning and activity—not by himself.

In these modern times, many will take these declarations very badly. Above all, The Arrogant Creative will take it the worst: which is to say, he'll do his darnedest to not take it at all.

BLINDSPOTS FOR THE CREATIVE ZM TYPE

THE ARROGANT CREATIVE

The Creative Type who lives in his financial blindspot, who is committed to self-deception, is trouble. These are fighting words, I know. Already we have encountered him in the relatively benign form of Old Broc. He is emotional and he is volatile. The Awake Creative is no choirboy, to be sure, but he knows that and has an excellent shot at catching himself before he ignites. But for The Arrogant Creative, personal money discussions, even mundane or in passing, can set him off. If The Creative is married, his spouse undoubtedly knows this. The trigger isn't just that he is emotional about his personal money. The trigger is that it's important for him to be important. Unlike "the millionaire next door," who relishes keeping count of what he has saved all these years, The Arrogant Creative cares about one thing: doing. Doing what he wants to do, when he wants to do it, and how he wants to do it—money be damned!

Reasonable? No, he's not reasonable to deal with, but he doesn't know that! The Arrogant Creative Type just doesn't see himself. His is an acute case of mistaken financial identity. Whether this is on purpose is debatable. His track record, however, is not. Blind to the messes he creates, he looks for quick fixes (i.e., refinance the house, take an untimely distribution from the retirement plan, spend the kids' college savings "just this once"...). Emotional volatility extends to managing investments. Of all the ZM Types, he is the most susceptible to "buy high and sell low," to call his broker and say "I want out of the market now," since he too often is swept away in the current of those ubiquitous market emotions: hope and fear. Successful investing is downright impossible if the investor gets emotional. And the Arrogant Creative gets emotional. Not that he sees that. He thinks he's being reasonable! Seriously. His arrogance and self-denial are trouble. They blind him to any sort of feedback and objective self-reflection. He's been going so hard and so long in a particular direction, it's extremely difficult to undo. And more often than not, it really is for him to undo. What Jana pulled off with Broc, in retrospect, was a small miracle. Thank God they loved each other.

The Arrogant Creative wholeheartedly believes what he thinks. Assumptive of his Hearth Money prowess, he believes he is a reasonable man. That his leaps of thought are at times erratic, that his financial logic may be patchwork—he has no suspicions about that. Again, this is a delicate matter. No one likes to be knocked around for how he thinks. It could get personal. Even so, The Creative, be he Arrogant or Awake or somewhere in between, is anything but objective and rational about his personal money. Not by himself, anyway. Often times, he just isn't making total sense. This really isn't that big a deal, if he has perspective and a sense of humor. Then the whole thing flips. Quite powerfully, I might add.

Personal money is best a social experience for The Creative.

You'll hear that mantra over and over. Then The Awake Creative can part ways with that big modern world fallacy of uber-individualism, and move back to the village. Or perhaps, move the village (his Money Mandala) to him. The beauty of this is compelling. Awake, his charisma is natural. He is receptive, intelligently so. People love that. There will be no issue of finding able helpers, when the time comes.

. . . .

THE AWAKE CREATIVE

The Arrogant Creative breaks the rules of personal finance —as a rule. This makes him a magnet for obstacles. The Awake Creative breaks the rules of personal finance—at the right time. This makes him a natural born risk taker. There's something to this. Deviating from the financial plan to assist the daughter who has gotten into medical school—this is a risk that lines up with the family values. The financial return on that "investment" may be modest, given the current economic environment for doctors and healthcare as a whole, but the personal and the social return may be huge, reverberating in many directions, felt for generations to come.

The Awake Creative has a canny moral compass. He is the guy who is most likely to refuse a gift or deal when it doesn't line up with his values or feel right. Others think he is crazy, but he couldn't care less. Money is not true north for The Awake Creative. His values are. His self-worth is not his net worth. Direction in life is abundantly clear to him. He has perspective in the grandest sense of the word. In other words, he knows the value of everything. Money will not lead him astray, although it could chronically distract him from his goal, if he fails to relate with it properly.

You may recall our earlier musings on The Maven and Oscar Wilde's Cynic: he knew the price of everything and the value of nothing. Well, the Awake Creative is aware that he has the potential in him to be the Cynic's kissin' cousin, the "Wise Fool"—to know the value of everything and the price of nothing. The Awake Creative knows that he is no Maven when it comes to price. The same could be said for his planning. And this is not for want of trying. Goodness knows, he's tried. And time and time again, he has displayed a propensity for mediocrity.

This gently penetrating awareness is the golden key for The Awake Creative. In this self-knowledge, he is humble yet dignified. He is open; able to be helped. This receptivity does not make The Creative a child. On the contrary, many a magnanimous and conquering king has succeeded, surrounded by the counsel of loyal able helpers. The king did not cook up the plans, but indeed he recognized the good plans. The king did not implement the plans, but indeed he recognized those who best could. More to come on this in Money Mandala Rx. For now, though, let it be said: The Awake Creative is well wired to make good use of that most precious resource of all: the human resource. He who is genuinely open to being helped, finds no shortage of deft wise folks who love to help. He creates his own self-regulating village. This is where The Creative's Type-in-action gets mighty interesting. This is where you can lavish him with praise.

Emotions Up!

Personal money is best a social experience for The Creative. Throwing off the shackles of the modern view of money and the individual, he therefore eschews isolation. This is good. For he is an emotional sort, The Creative. And while he can be a most excellent judge of the counsel he receives from others regarding

Hearth Money affairs, he will do well to have a sense of humor and rather spacious view of things that dawn in his own mind. Wiring is wiring. That doesn't go away. Remember The Great Hunter in the mythic village, the one who cannot be outdone on the hunt, but who nonetheless habitually burns the meat when cooking and has since been relegated to dish duty? Well, don't think for a second that he doesn't pine about getting back to the kitchen, back to the stove, back to the skewer sticks. Indeed, he pines; and indeed, the village elders say: *No can do.*

Thoughts are powerful, especially emotional thoughts, fueling all manner of word and action. This can be good, bad, neutral, or other. You see this same energetic flow in The Good Book, with its focus on "thought, word, and deed." And, it's the same with money. Money is a great catalyst of the emotions. Add in a conductor, The Creative Type, the most emotional of them all. Moving at lightening speed, with tremendous strength, this is his train: thoughts>emotions>words>action. It moves fast.

Emotions vivify and color experience. The price of emotions is objectivity. Nonetheless, happy emotions should still be your friend, right? Well, maybe. Actually, in the land of personal finance, not so much. The Creative is just plain vulnerable to being led around by his fear and being led around by his euphoria. All roads lead to anxiety and distraction, until he gets really solid and grounded in managing his Hearth Money world. It's easy to see how messing up on the big things will decimate you, but for The Creative, it's more often than not the compilation of all the small things.

I think the dining out culture is a good case in point. Boulder is a town renowned for big sky and beautiful mountains and an exceptionally high number of restaurants. The modern world is stressful, no doubt about it; and, like other folks, The Creative

Type is wont to come home and say, *I'm exhausted. Worked my butt off all day at the office. Let's go out for a bite.* Or, there is the more cheerful version of this: *Darlin', I had a great day at the office. Did us proud. Let's go out and celebrate right now!* And indeed, celebrating or decompressing may be just what's called for. Only there's this one itty-bitty sobering issue, which should confront The Creative, but probably won't (till much later):

> Can they really afford to be doing this? This dinner
> for two, with wine and dessert and tip and cigar and
> valet parking? This dinner out which looks an awful
> lot like a host of other dinners out?

The Creative here doesn't have a clue. Yes, it's true that he doesn't have some big attitude about himself and money. He knows he's no Archer. He's just greatly relieved to kick some butt at work, or decompress, or whatever. But as for the budget, well, no, he doesn't have a clue. He doesn't have that information handy. Nor does he think about it…till later!

And this leaves The Creative—a happy camper earlier in the evening—with a nasty hangover later on: money anxiety. For when The Creative spends his money or invests his money, too often he really doesn't know if he is applying it in the right direction. Even if he wanted the information, chances are he'd never find it. Too often, his world is not set up this way. He's making decisions based on best guesses, or no guesses at all. This is a shame, a veritable standing invite to that great thief who later steals the evening: money anxiety.

The Awake Creative is no stranger to money anxiety. In fact, he could write the book on money anxiety, based on his previous incarnation as an unconscious Creative. This is why he no longer freewheels in isolation. Or at least tries not to. Financial planning has become a great ally. This includes working a budget. I know, it's so dang basic. But the basics never get old, and the benefits are tangible. Top of the planning benefits list is this: when The Creative spends his money, he knows that that is definitely what he should do with it—spend such and such an amount on groceries, clothes, gifts, etc.. Spend it and feel good about that. And when his money is to be saved, and allocated to investments to accomplish certain goals, he knows that that is precisely what he should do with those funds—invest in college education, retirement, give the kids a down payment for the first house. This is one of the great, if not truly simple joys in the land of Hearth Money. With a little help from his friends, The Creative consistently knows when to spend and feel the goodness of that, and when to invest and feel the goodness of that. Accordingly, he is not fated to personal money anxiety. On the contrary, the Awake Creative is now poised for blessing and wealth in the largest sense of the term.

THE CONTROVERSIAL CREATIVE ZM TYPE—REDUX

Can't plan? Can't implement? Are you sure? How can this be? The Creative Type is not dim-witted, spaced out, or rebellious, though he may be "misunderstood." As you already know, he can count, looks like you and me, might be pretty well educated, might even be an accomplished hunter, but his planning and implementing are mediocre. In the routine of personal money life, he's not a complete no-show. More likely, he's not much of an initiator. His spark comes from and through relationships. Personal finance is best a social experience for him. Time to go to the store: he's willing to make a list with you. He'll be the scribe, and be sure to add his favorite black tea and Newman's Own®

cookies and other items to the list. Time to buy a car: you can give him detailed instructions on which sales guy to talk to, which car, which package, at what price; but don't expect him to come home victorious like The Maven. He'll do an OK job, but nothing like The Maven. His heart isn't that into the big back-and-forth negotiation. He knows it and the sales guy will know it. You should know it, too.

Entrusting the family books to him—this is not such a good idea. He might agree to do it, but then, when the moment arrives and it's time to figure out if you can really go out to dinner, don't waste your time looking for current budget-tracker info. It won't be there! Updates will be irregular, at best. The bigger the personal financial decision, the bigger the mistake it is to let him freewheel in isolation. The bigger the personal financial decision, the more emotional it is for The Creative, particularly one who operates in isolation. Heaven forbid he is unilaterally in charge of family finances. Sounds like it might be time for a *coup*. But not-in-isolation, The Creative is invaluable, becoming a storehouse for all sorts of Maven gems on Costco and travel, continuing ed and pottery classes, fiction and movies, and you get the point. What's more, The Awake Creative smartly vets through The Mavenry Nation, identifying the folks and blogs who share his aesthetic taste, his values, and (dare I say it!) his price point. The Creative's route is always going to be circuitous, never direct, in the land of Hearth Money. Makes for an interesting journey, if you ask me.

EMOTIONS DOWN!

Money in and of itself doesn't have special meaning for The Creative. In fact, this is the Type most likely to see the "energetic baggage" on gifts or inheritances. Not long ago, a woman called me to see if I could help her. We met and she told me the story of her family and its social rise and fall, and her push-pull relation-ship to the trust company, and what she did when at last her Mom died and her funds were released from trust.

Now mind you this is an educated, cultured, articulate woman. But emotional about the family money? Well, consider what she told me: *After Mom died, I quit my job, and traveled and shopped and gave it away. I could not be rid of my inheritance fast enough. I was angry and hurt, and it felt good to be sending away this thing— this exasperating two million dollars—that my Mom perpetually jerked me around with. It was pure rebellion on my part and it felt great. But now there's a pittance left and that feels like hell. I'm scared. But truth be told, I don't regret spending a penny of it. I detest what that money stood for.*

This might strike you as extreme, but it is exceptionally emo-tionally honest. You might say, *What a fool!* But then let's stop and take stock. This sort of behavior happens all the time. Ask the Trust Officer at the bank. She'll tell you. Most inheritances will be gone within 18 months of people receiving them. Yikes! Talk about emotional money—and the countless real or perceived messages riding on that money.

So while a catharsis may be just what the patient ordered, it's not what the financial advisor ordered. Nor what *Zen Money Blues* ordered. Get that mythic village around The Creative ASAP! Emotions are fast, powerful, and propel all manner of action. Personal money is best a social experience. In the village, he can air his disgruntlements, his injustices, or the joy of his triumphs, but his Money Mandala people will do him a great favor by con-sistently inviting him to decouple emotions from his money. Clearly emotions can breathe color and life into experience. Any experience. Loving his children. Buying a parcel of land to build on. Listening to beautiful melancholic music. Emotions and money, however, are a volatile combo, and can lead to some pretty weird stuff. Besides, *Zen Money Blues* is clear on this point: frittering away what he has is rarely going to be medicinal. Plainly, there are better ways to mend a broken heart.

. . . .

THELONIUS ROCKEFELLER

Money—as in what he has in the bank or investments or real estate or jewelry or cars—is not The Awake Creative's primary measure of success. He could be worth tens of millions or decidedly middle class or living jazz-gig to jazz-gig. His measuring stick is broad and assuredly has depth. This is where things actually make sense. Since The Creative Type isn't sitting around making all sorts of plans or dreaming of heroic Maven activities, he's got a little time on his hands to think of all the other things. Wiring is wiring. For the Awake Creative, his personal finance abilities might be mediocre but his moral compass is not. "Success" means great affirmation of life. Success is perspective. Success is balance. Success possesses some combination of health and love and family and friends and Nature and inspired life's work and literature and banter of storytelling and endless games and a host of other "non-money" things. Arguably, this is what makes The Creative the perfect match for The Archer. In the land of Hearth Money, The Awake Creative creates his circle of helpers and thereby takes responsibility. All is circuitous, processed in relationship, and it works. Diana's different. She is direct, like a whistling arrow flying at the target. So, if you'll excuse me, I have an introduction to make: *Thelonius Rockefeller, meet Diana The Archer!*

PITH SUMMARY OF THE CREATIVE ZM TYPE
PLANNER: NO. IMPLEMENTER: NO.

Chapter 11

ZM Type Four:

THE ARCHER

NICKNAME: DIANA
PLANNER: YES. IMPLEMENTER: YES.

Note: By now you can hear the *Zen Money Blues* groove in your head, and perhaps in your sleep. Nonetheless, kindly allow me to make a humble recapitulation. Yes, The Archer is the poster-child for personal finance, albeit in the conventional view of things. That conventional view is respected up to a point. Her prowess is to be admired, though like the other ZM Types, she has her vulnerabilities and her humanity, not to mention her responsibilities. The *Zen Money Blues* paradigm salutes but does not exalt any one ZM Type. Each Type has a part to play. Each Type, when managed well, is worthy of tremendous respect. So the game is not to turn anyone into something she is not. Wiring is wiring. The Creative can't become The Archer no matter how hard he tries; nor, for that matter, can The Archer become The Creative. Equanimity is perhaps the supreme *Zen Money Blues* virtue. That, I believe, is worth holding in mind.

OK, now the time has come to give The Archer her due.

THE ARCHER—DIANA

The Archer has the prescience of The Architect and the means and daring of The Maven, and something more. She can plan and she can implement, and the whole is greater than the sum of the parts. You know the expression 2 + 2 = 5? The Archer functions like that. She can see the target and she can hit the target, but what is truly remarkable is her ability to bide her time, and strike at the perfect moment. Be in the moment? Yes. Plan with a short-to-intermediate term view? Yes. Plan with a long view? But, of course. The Archer goes direct.

That being said, her weapons and her skill often abide in the shadows of self-secrecy. She may be the last to know that she herself is The Archer, if she ever knows. The modern world is no help. It is rife with those who overestimate their personal money capabilities, who assert their competence at every turn, yet they are the faux-Archers, passing off mania and activity as skill. Everyday wisdom puts a gender spin on this: men tend to overestimate their personal money skills and women tend to underestimate theirs. Perhaps. It seems to be true, but I'm not ready to add that to the file labeled "Wild Speculations In Need of Defending."

Meanwhile, The Archer-in-the-shadows subplot makes for decent copy. It reads like a Superhero coming-of-age story. Out of touch with the fact that she has the complete Archer package—bow, arrow, quiver, fleet foot, and discerning eye that sees gainful targets—the talents of The Archer lie dormant. Life goes on. Society, parents, spouse, siblings don't suspect a thing. Then a cataclysmic event happens: divorce, disability, death of partner or parents. Now she must discover her powers. She must train herself in the ways of The Archer and put those powers to good use, for the benefit of herself and others. It's a little corny, this Superhero plot line, except that this is real life and it happens all the time.

ZEITGEIST

Women, in particular, seem to intuit that this plot line may be their own. As if moved by the winds of the 21st century American *zeitgeist*, it seems that women *en masse* are training themselves in the ways of The Archer. Such training will not turn negative, in fact will be quite beneficial, as long as the participants recognize that most of them are not The Archer of personal finance. Same goes for men. Just ask Broc! Just ask Elephant Hunter! Given this ZM reality, these women can then incorporate pieces of the training, empowering their natural strengths and adroitly managing and containing the rest. Those who need to make personal finance a social experience, will do just that. No big deal.

Typically more advisor-receptive, women consistently seek out two things in a relationship with a financial advisor. One is education. The other is a "thought-partner." The former grounds them, orients them to the lay of the land, of planning and implementing. The latter offers them an intelligent, objective person with whom they can think things through, take action, and monitor and evaluate their strategy and action in a safe and contained way. Given the apparent reality that a disproportionate amount of inherited wealth seems to be flowing to women, this is timely indeed.

The high end of popular culture is hip to this 21st century American *zeitgeist*. In year four of HBO's *The Sopranos*, the irrepressible Carmella—wife of the uncanny underworld boss, Tony—has an awakening. Death and uncertainty surround her family's life, vividly so, and she wants some security, some peace of mind, but she knows nothing about what assets they have and where things are, in case something should happen to Tony (a not unlikely prospect given his line of work). He, in classic old school fashion, tells her: *You'll be taken care of, if something happens to me. That's all you gotta know.* This placates her not at all. She talks with the previous mob boss's wife, Rosalie, after a church luncheon, and inquires about how well she has been taken care of since her husband's death. Carmella receives a less than reassuring, *Well, it's OK, I guess.* And then Rosalie catches herself and dismisses it, *But you know: how much is enough anyways!*

Carmella is on a mama-bear jag. She is a whistling arrow destined for the target. There's no stopping her now. Her cousin's son, Brian, is a financial planner, with whom Carmella has several educative discussions. Daily, she devours the business section and tunes into CNBC. She's boning up on trusts, revocable and irrevocable, as well as blue chip stocks and IRS reporting requirements for putting cash into a brokerage account. Carmella means business, and makes it abundantly clear to Tony that *this is important to me.* He of course procrastinates, which puts him in the doghouse. The flow of good food and cheerful company comes to an icy halt. Tony, probably a Creative ZM Type, acts smartly in ZM character. He summons one of his outside counselors to golf, where he gets the lowdown on the trusts (one yes, one no) and returns home ready to go with a portion of Carmella's plan. Peace is restored.

RINZAI POUNDING ON THE DOOR

While Carmella had her awakening triggered by the tragic loss in a friend's family, Kathy wasn't so lucky. What's more, Kathy is no fictional character. Her fall was intimately tied to the fall of her husband (William), and his fall was intimately tied to the fall of his company stock. Every advisor in the business has one of these stories. I will tell you mine. The term in the investment management industry is "concentrated stock position." The term is synonymous with risk—the bad kind. There are some very solid strategies to manage this risk. Whether William eschewed strategy or just plain got bum advice still isn't clear—probably a combination of the two—but this much is clear: back in the day (the '01-'02 Bear Market) William was paralyzed with fear, sick with anxiety, and not surprisingly, did absolutely nothing amidst the serious danger. Unfortunately Kathy colluded, and "went along," as if there were meaning to this madness, producing a toxic concoction for their personal money.

William blew it, no doubt about it. But shine the light on Kathy, I must. Why? Because she colluded. How did she collude? She abdicated her Archer Type mojo. Why did she do that? She wishes she knew. Here is what I understand went down. Early on in their marriage they established some rules around personal money. It seems that among the many dynamics between them, one centered on Kathy's fear of being a "controlling b-tch" to William. Hence, they made this agreement: *You handle your money, I'll handle mine, and we'll negotiate the shared aspects of our financial life each step of the way.* Seems reasonable enough. Except the truth of ZM wiring screws everything up.

William is a slightly dreamy biotech researcher/inventor/ entrepreneur, who is also The Creative ZM Type. Kathy knows personal money, through and through—a classic Archer. The agreement between them was ill wrought. It was a contract for disaster.

Collusion goes in the "one eye open" category. There is a feeling of haze. You suspect something's wrong, but you just don't feel brave enough to blow the whistle on yourself—to speak your wisdom. You're strangely attached to the neurotic setup. You hear Rinzai knocking on the door. You hear him pounding and making a racket. Rude zen wants in. Is this a bad dream? You don't know what to make of it all, and in the last analysis do nothing.

After William's company stock rose exponentially; after they went from net worth of $4M to net worth of $11M; after William eschewed the whispery counsel of his advisors; after their net worth streaked back to earth, leaving a million-dollar house and Kathy's diversified million-dollar portfolio still standing but William's stock almost worthless; after Kathy bore witness to it all and stood among the ruins, or remembered the ruins—these words (her words) burned the air:

I knew better. I knew we were fools, and I let him do it.

One eye had been open. She had known better. She had stood by, silently complicit. Even now, I can hear Rinzai stark raving mad. Kathy's betrayal was personal. It was betrayal of the self by the self. At the moment of truth, she refused herself permission to shoot. To let loose her arrows. This is the portrait of the Archer before she comes into her own. This is The Archer's archenemy.

GRANDMA DROVE A GREEN VOLKSWAGEN BEETLE

"Injury to the light" is an expression from the Tao, and there can be no doubt this is what William and Kathy experienced. Thankfully, not every Archer Type has to go through hell to get to the treasures that were always her own. My Irish grandmother was one such person. From what I can surmise, she and my grandfather (also Irish immigrant) found their groove from the get-go. When he had work, which was sporadic in the early years of The Great Depression, he brought home what he made and gave it to Grandma. She had a houseful of little people and she held the family purse, and when needed, which was often, she worked outside the home to make ends meet. In 1940, they moved 25 miles north, from the Manhattan East Side neighborhood near Columbia Presbyterian Hospital up to Rye, which was the country then. There Grandpa opened a produce stand. Grandma episodically worked as nanny for a couple of wealthy families who lived in the big houses on the country club grounds, and of course raised her own children. The personal money drill remained the same. Grandpa turned over what he had to Grandma, who doled it out as she saw fit. I don't know if lots of folks did it that way or not back then. What I do know is that their story of struggle and modest means was common. The Irish were one group among many, making their way through a period of prolonged slump and obstacles that not many of us can relate to now, even if—in historical terms—we're only talking about the blink of an eye: 65-75 years ago.

Which brings me back to my Irish grandmother. I can't tell you stories of how she planned like Terra, or negotiated innumerable deals like The Maven, because I never knew her in that way. She was my rotund, loving, Irish grandmother, who served tea with milk and sugar for any malady, which really did make me feel better afterward. She picked me up for the early church service, in her 1968 green Volkswagen Bug, which had four on the floor (yes, Grandma drove a stick). But for Grandma, the proof was in the pudding. She had six children, of whom five (one died young) went on to be extraordinarily successful and fulfilled in their lives and careers. Though the means were modest, and at times scarce, Grandma clearly had known how to get the right stuff (education, clothes, manners, values) into the psycho-emotional "backpack" of each one of her children, who then went out into the world and made something awesome of their lives. Family bragging aside, I really do think of my Irish grandmother as one of those extraordinary people who quietly led an extraordinary life. Somehow circumstances and personalities lined up, such that in her family, her Archer skills were always in action and never in doubt. Like the biblical miracles of the wine at the wedding feast and the loaves of bread and the fishes, Grandma made a little go a long way.

And that is the magic of The Archer Type. It is alchemical magic. When everything comes together, the whole is greater than the sum of the parts. It could be timing, insight, luck. Doesn't matter, really. What matters is that The Archer is active, leading from the front, yet not afraid to do the scut work when needed. Then luck and skill and timing and circumstance align. Both eyes open, The Archer can't miss. That is, of course, unless she is blinded by that all-too-human emotion, the catalyst of tragedy—pride!

BLINDSPOTS FOR THE ARCHER ZM TYPE

HUBRIS

Dynamics in couples and across family generations is a fascinating area. This certainly is true with the ZM Types. Just as The Architect and The Maven are opposites, potentially complementing or conflicting, so it is with The Archer and The Creative Types. This can be a terrific match made in heaven, or sheer hell, depending on roles and responsibilities, and on who leads and who follows. The knock on the full grown, come-in-to-her-own Archer Type is that she can be judgmental. Contemptuous is another adjective that comes to mind—contemptuous that others aren't as competent and effective as she is in managing her personal financial affairs. You see this play out in marriages and families all the time. Mainstream literature on personal finance, sadly, adds fuel to this fire. Rendering its own list of unhelpful demands on and judgments about non-Archer Types, it perpetuates the dysfunction.

In that mythic village, when John J. Hunter III performed abysmally in his cooking duties, the elders reassigned him to dish detail or some such. The village was self-regulating. In modern times, the myth of the uber-individual prevails, and that includes the impractical belief that each individual should be a good hunter, a good purse manager, not to mention a lady and a scholar. The Archer, in the realm of personal finance, is enormously gifted. John J. Hunter III is not. Communicating displeasure that he is "irresponsible, jejune, weak-willed, doltish, rebellious, incompetent, and otherwise screwed up," will not remedy the situation. Will not be a means to empowerment. Rather, it has the opposite effect. It lets the John III's-of-the-world off the hook. After all, if you're a screw up, what's the point anyway?

Pride is not a one size fits all proposition. The Archer has good reason to feel proud. The problem is when it goes too far. This could be based on resentment that she often carries a significantly heavier load than the other ZM Types. However, this could be an erroneous view. Nature gives gifts, and those gifts have requirements. Well endowed, The Archer must exercise her chops, circulate, and stay sharp; or risk falling back into an unproductive dormant state. This is not to say that, for example, The Archer is meant to clean up mess after mess made by Old Broc. No, not at all. Rather, it's to say that hard work goes, hand in glove, with her enormous talent. She is illustrious, and deserving of all the recognition and honor that come her way.

When pride gets righteous, however, this is not good. Judgment becomes high-handed, and puts a nasty stink on the family money. Our Creative friend, the one who vomited up a large portion of her $2M inheritance, could soliloquize on the matter. These judgments are extremely powerful. I don't think The Archer, as parent or spouse, has any idea how powerful these judgments are. Therefore, The Archer should consider another plan of attack, if she is displeased with the actions of those around her. Rather than demand that they be like her or face the wrath of judgment, perhaps she could encourage them to mature in light of their financial identities—their ZM Types. Get them to take responsibility for that. This is fair game.

Gardenia

In Hearth Money matters, The Archer is accomplishing. Fully grown, she needs no one. But there's that not so small matter called life. In this regard, The Awake Creative may be a great friend to her. Often chaotic, he nonetheless has a canny knack for knowing that line, where "money" ends and "non-money" begins. Knowing that line may not be The Archer's strong suit. A subtle version of Wilde's Cynic looms for her. There's a tendency to reduce all things to something she knows and is very good at: personal money. It's human nature. Still and all, she should desist from doing that. Not a winning habit. Besides, the benefits of desisting are considerable. Money won't seep into every nook of her life and relationships. This is good. Nor will she accidentally overlook the non-money gifts from her children and spouse and friends. This is important. Then money will occupy its proper place, and not interfere in the bedroom, nor be a stone in the backpacks of those precious ones who carry her name and good works with them, as they go out to make their way in the world. Now her money will be fragrant, like a gardenia—as any of us would want it to be.

SERMON ON THE MOUNT

Life is big. Money is no more than a piece of it. If The Archer's aim is to build a multigenerational family dynasty, gathering power so that she and generations of her progeny can heal and lead the world, then some real thought needs to go into what is transmitted across generations. Making her children into what they are not with regards to Hearth Money, just isn't going to work. It's futile, and will likely create the opposite result. So she should go with what is. Work with their brilliance, and encourage maturity with the weak spots. Cultivate what is there. Or, as that Great Anointed Sage once said: *Be generous in spirit.*

I've known some sweet, tender, very kind Archers, and I've known some cold, parsimonious, hard-to-love Archers. I've known Archers who've consistently thought of family and friends and community and onward, and I've known Archers who've thought of no one but themselves. Doubtless there are many in between. But the bottom line question for The Archer, is this:

How magnanimous will you choose to be?

There's Self and then there's self. The Archer has a legitimate sphere of influence. Her words matter. Her frown matters. Her smile matters. Being generous in spirit is a conscious decision for her to make.

. . . .

DIANA

Diana the Archer has the complete package. Her journey is straight as an arrow, with tidy and explosive self-growth phases. First, she has to have her awakening (*I am The Archer—dang it!*). Second, there is The Education of The Archer. She drinks up expert advice on planning and implementing from every imaginable quarter, and she will, if she puts her mind to it. Which leads to number three: she needs to activate herself, each and every day. Her level of understanding and activity should be that of the master. Nothing else will do. She is stable, clear, and thorough. She gets the big picture and she gets the nuance. And like no other Type, she knows detachment. She is a cool customer. That may be her greatest asset. But once arrived, she will do well not to commit her own version of the fallacy of overreaching. Beware! Money is great, but life is so much bigger. Mastery of money is simply mastery of money. Essential but not sufficient. Kindness and gratitude are virtues. Diana mustn't let the power of her ZM gift turn into her nemesis.

PITH SUMMARY OF THE ARCHER ZM TYPE
PLANNER: YES. IMPLEMENTER: YES.

Chapter 12 ZM Types and You

W HO ARE YOU? WHICH ZM Type are you? By now
this may be abundantly clear. Or perhaps it is abundantly
clear that your spouse is X-Type, but maybe not as clear what Type
you are. Narrative and story are illuminating for some, but not for
others. Hence, *Zen Money Blues* cordially invites back my very
proper 8th grade English teacher, Miss Herald. She's on a test giving
bender, and it seems like it might be useful to shine a light on her
method and her madness. The ZM Type Quiz is a three-pronged
approach, a trident if you will, that analyzes Action, Emotion,
and Effectiveness amid **planning and implementing.**

Two questions loom: Are you a planner? Are you an implementer? Accurately answer those two questions and you're home
free to your ZM identity—who you are before you write a check,
shop for food, poke through the sales rack, or pull out of your
pocket that wad of hundreds (or fistful of scrunched up ones and
fives). Action is behavior. Emotions are psychological. Effectiveness is results. Let's study each more closely, before Miss Herald
makes her move.

ACTION

Cast aside intentionality. Of course your intentions are noble and decent and good. It doesn't matter here. What counts is making a study of your financial self-in-action: what you do, how you do it, and what you don't do. Behavior is the word. The question is NOT: Can you plan? Can you implement? Rather: How well do you plan? How well do you implement?

The tracks of the past are worth following. Do you know what it costs to live your life? Kind of, or for real? How consistently do you keep tabs on this? How do you follow your investments? Do brokerage statements get opened? What are your main financial goals? How clear and detailed are they? Can you articulate them now? Would your spouse/partner agree? When shopping, do you find the deals? Do you look at the price tag? Shop with a budget line in mind? What about plans for the unexpected—disability, death, or long-term care? Is your will in line with your wishes? Do you have a will? How current are you on guardianship issues? Follow-through is a big issue for some. How often do you know what you need to do, and just don't do it? When you start a financial project, do you in fact bring it to completion?

Before you compare notes with your spouse, parents, children; before you activate their perspective on your history of actions—take a nice, long look in the mirror. The mirror of past and present. Consider your track record as planner and as implementer. Look. Take a long look, but do not judge. Just look and see. The second coming of Miss Herald and The ZM Type Quiz aspire to help. Aspire to be that good, clear, undistorted mirror. Therefore, do give these matters your attention. Bring them into focus. The tracks of your past actions cannot be that hard to make out. You're living in their midst. Follow them. It will pay dividends.

EMOTION

Next, link that track record with emotion, which is kind of like tuning in to the *Zen Money Blues* soundtrack while taking a self-polygraph test. How do you feel when you pay the bills, or get the dinner check, or see your investments going up or down? How do you feel when you don't do something you suspect you should—like pay the bills, open the investment statements, or update that bloody Quicken program that you started nine months ago? Are you feeling bitchy, intimidated, cheerful, depressed, numb, bored, pissed, parsimonious, magnanimous, industrious, manic, soporific, other? How do you really feel?

Sometimes it helps to look on objectively, as if you were a disinterested third party, noting the emotions of that Chap over there: Oh yes, him, over there, at table nine. Nice enough looking fellow, though he appears a wee bit queasy now that he's foolishly played the hero, having picked up the dinner tab and learned what kind of wine bill his rowdy old prep school friends racked up this night! It gets worse. The wife—his wife—is seething. He'll have an eternity of hell to pay, which includes not getting any later in the evening! Feeling: you want to know what he's feeling. I'll tell you what our Foolish Hero is feeling: he's feeling wretched.

Or noting the emotions of this Fine Lady here: Dear me, yes, that smart looking lady, with the salt-and-pepper hair, lurching over the bills atop her antique desk. She's in a swivet. A bona fide swivet. Seems she forgot exactly how much she spent at Saks the other day—a few weeks ago, whenever it was. It was such a triumphant day for her: beautiful clothes, one of a kind jewelry—unpretentious, genuine *objets d'art*! And Saks, what a spot, with refreshing A/C and bubbly Perrier® to drink between donning outfits, and, well, that American Express® bill in her hand cannot be right, can it? Feeling: you want to know what she's feeling? I'll tell you what our Grand Dame is feeling: she's furious, mostly with herself.

EFFECTIVENESS

The red herrings of quotidian reality abound. *This Zen Money Type stuff is beneath me! I know how to write a check, balance a checkbook, and invest my life's savings in penny stocks!* Jesting aside, this no doubt is true. Any ZM Type can do any given thing in personal finance. Nothing is that hard anyway. Balance a checkbook, pay a bar tab, comprehend the basic tenets of a Family Revocable Trust, choose a mutual fund, read a Value Line report, file your taxes online, and so on: these are the activities of the personal finance domain. All are knowable. What's more, only you can judge if you're feeling deeply resentful reconciling the checkbook or feeling averse to haggling with a car salesman over price. Of course, your spouse or family members might have something to say about your outbursts or nonstop biting remarks. But still and all, you are the last and the best and only honest judge of how you feel, unless of course incongruous actions start to drown out your words.

Effectiveness is that test of congruity. It's where rock meets bone. Beyond intentions, beyond what you can do, beyond how you feel: How often have you actually lived in budget? Saved according to plan? Bought the right house at the right price? Steered clear of volatile emotions? Let money become a divisive family issue? How in fact have the investments done? How many times have you gotten in the way? Gotten out of the way? Heeded good counsel? Brushed aside good counsel? Relative to what you have brought home, is your personal balance sheet ("net worth") underwhelming? Overwhelming? Just about what it should be? What position does money occupy in your life? Too distracting?

Still in the bedroom? Just the right spot?

ACTION, EMOTION, EFFECTIVENESS: BE WHO YOU ARE

This is the bad news and the good news of *Zen Money Blues*: most of us have no business handling our personal finances the way we do. We're wasting our time, our money, our relationships, our life force. We can do the right actions and get okay results, and yet generate such a mountain of misery that we make ourselves sick, or drive our spouse and kids nuts, or habitually wake up in the middle of the night and watch the action on the Tokyo Markets on Bloomberg, or worry about things over which we have little control (and at that time of night absolutely no control over). We can't get around our personal financial identity, till we get it right. And then we own it. We stop the fight and the tussle, and are able to see before us something quite remarkable: the path of least resistance. It's about letting round rocks roll downhill, which is what they want to do. The key is to get in a position such that the round rocks are at the hilltop. Then, let them go. When we see clearly and own our particular ZM Type, then we can organize our world so that our money has the opportunity to generate harmony and peace and nourishment and of course prosperity in our world. This is *Zen Money Blues*. We ride the natural power of our money.

Uppp—no more time for prep or riffing on the path of least resistance. Here she comes, standing tall, papers in hand. It's time for the test. She's passing them out, while humming the faintest of tunes. Very hard to make out, but—whoa, very cool. She's quietly jamming on some electric blues: "In My Time of Dying."[5] And then the humming stops, and Miss Herald utters her favorite pre-exam phrase: *Break a leg!*

THE ZM TYPE QUIZ

The Quiz aims to answer the two most fundamental questions of personal money: Are you a planner? Are you an implementer? Below is a reminder of what that yields in the ZM Typology.

THE ZM MATRIX:
WHO YOU ARE WITH YOUR HEARTH MONEY

	Plan	Implement
The Architect (Celeste and Terra)	Yes	No
The Maven (New York)	No	Yes
The Creative (Thelonius Rockefeller)	No	No
The Archer (Diana)	Yes	Yes

MISS HERALD'S QUIZ INSTRUCTIONS:

Quite on purpose, this quiz is short. However, there's a catch. You need to take it twice. First take it by yourself, and then take it with someone else. As you hear throughout *Zen Money Blues*, for many of us, money is best a social experience. In that spirit, do your best to take in what your friend/spouse/parent/sibling or other significant person has to say. Pay close attention to areas that diverge from your own view of yourself. Lively dialogue is ideal. Or, to use a word from the Socratic method: Dialecticate!

Are You a Planner?

This is a simple yet ticklish question, because the planner has multiple expressions, all of them valid. If in fact you are a planner, then you will most likely embody one of these three expressions (though a hybrid expression is possible): the Celestial Planner, the Terra Planner, or the Walden Pond Planner. Therefore, taking this quiz will be most meaningful if you have perused the ways of the planner as described in The Architect ZM Type chapter.

If you are a planner, your answers will be "yes" regarding the spirit of the statements. There should be resonance.

1. I do consistently make plans in my mind or on paper. This is my nature. Plans might be about family gatherings, beauty, largesse, adventure, social amity (like Celeste); or practical in nature, managing menu and kids and house and job, along with adventure and family or social connectivity (like Terra); or coveting simplicity (like Walden Pond). My plans have a time element, for sure. It could be upgrading to a bigger house in the next couple of years so friends and family can come and stay at our place, or it could be starting the college fund upon the birth of our children, or keeping life simple so I can go back to India for 3 months this winter. In short, there is a definite design element to my world, which includes my personal finances. I don't need prompting from other people to be this way; this is how I am.

2. I really enjoy making plans. I enjoy the big picture of the plan; the details of the plan; or the simplicity of the plan.

3. I'm good at designing my world. Whether Celeste or Terra style, I'm quite organized and effective at this.

€

Are You An Implementer?

If you are an implementer, your answers will be "yes" regarding the spirit of the statements. There should be resonance.

1. I understand price. I don't buy food, clothes, cars, plane tickets, etc. without having checked and compared prices. Negotiating I do without hesitation. Paying bills and squirreling away money and staying on top of my money isn't hard for me. I tune into the special knowledge of other Mavens. This is a consistent mode of operating for me. I naturally work this way.

2. I love a deal. I thoroughly enjoy "Mavenizing" pretty much every important purchase, and sometimes even small purchases. Getting a good deal is very important to me. Other people can pay full retail, but not me!

3. I'm an excellent, effective purchaser of travel, fun, toys, food, and experiences. No doubt about it, I consistently possess Maven prowess. Research and comparison shopping are often part of the process; this is time well spent, in my book.

. . . .

Miss Herald's After-Quiz Commentary

This quiz is meant to be a social experience. Spirited dialogue is such an effective way to shine a light on the blindspots that we all possess. In the end, with a little help from your friends, you are the final judge on this matter.

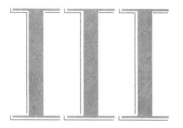

THE
Rx OF MONEY
MANDALA

Chapter 13 Money Mandala:
Managing Your ZM Type

MANDALA MEANS "CIRCLE" in Sanskrit. Nothing mystical is intended here. Carl Jung wrote essays on mandala drawings and paintings, as they appeared in Tibetan Buddhism and Tantric Hinduism and as they spontaneously appeared in the drawings of his patients. Jung was intrigued and noted that this activity of creating mandalas had the effect of restoring a certain psychic balance in the patient. In the land of *Zen Money Blues*, creating your own personal Money Mandala has parallel efficacy: you establish and maintain your Money Mandala to keep your personal financial world refreshed and in balance.

Mandala here connotes earthy and practical: literally, visualizing and gathering around you your circle of people, and then expanding out, to include whatever resources you have. Heretofore, *Zen Money Blues* has made this oft-repeated assertion: for many folks, personal money is best a social experience. Hence, Money Mandala. You are creating a humble prototype of the mythic village, with a thoroughly modern twist. Your ZM Type qualities (strengths and weaknesses) are what they are, so go with the flow and manage them accordingly. The hard part is shining a light on your own Type. The easy part is creating the appropriate Money Mandala, where you get what you need: activation, information, affirmation, or counsel. This is the merry part, even if there is the occasional heavy lifting. Money Mandala doesn't require scads of money to create, though it is worth making some investment in. What's more, once you get your personal finance house in order, you tend to make oodles more money (Hunter activity). Why this is so, goes in the file for "Wild Speculations To Be Elaborated On One Day." In the meantime, let it be. It just is. Experience and story, again and again, corroborate this beneficial truth.

At the heart center of this Mandala is you. That is the ruling position. You set things in motion. You are the one responsible for what comes to pass. Speckled throughout Money Mandala Rx's are references to "your sovereign." Sometimes you'll see "sovereign-ness" used interchangeably. Sovereign is inseparable from your willfulness, literally "what you want and what you aim for." Sovereign acknowledges that you are the prime mover and beneficiary of this Money Mandala. You are the driver. The sovereign occupies the very center of the mandala.

But there is an interesting twist. Not all sovereigns work the same. The mechanics are different, at least in the land of the ZM Types. Some sovereigns are process-oriented; should push major financial decisions through a circuitous route, which includes gathering excellent information and counsel from their Money Mandala people; and then act, or delegate. Others move through the world, poised. They see the target, recognize the opportunity, and let fly—unerringly—in a moment's notice. The moment is the fruition of a thousand pieces of preparation. Both of these are expressions of sovereign-ness, yet are very different. The former is so named the "yin sovereign." Yin connotes receptivity, inviting in counsel and information, and holding that counsel and information, before acting. The latter is the "yang sovereign," because this mode of ruling is direct and immediate and overtly powerful. As ever, one style is not better than another. Each has its discernable patterns and its nuance. In popular culture, the dominant portrayal of someone in a leading role still tends to be, after all these years, the yang sovereign. Highly prized is the can-do, take-charge, get-it-done, will-oneself-to-victory kind of guy or gal. This might make for a more exciting movie or sporting event, but in real life it makes for bad personal money drama, unless of course this is in line with your personal financial identity.

I recognize that already you have worked hard to acculturate to the land of ZM Typology, and now I am laying on you a conceptual slice of India and Tibet, followed by a razor thin exegesis on the cosmic polarities of yin and yang. Please breathe out and relax. Miss Herald has retired for the evening. There is no pop quiz imminent. I promise you I am not the money doctor who writes prescriptions in indecipherable chicken scratch. It just seemed a courtesy to get you familiar with the expanded *Zen Money Blues* lexicon. And in the next four chapters, where you will indeed find a clearly written prescription for each of the four ZM Types, this will surely come in handy.

Chapter 14

THE ARCHITECT'S MONEY MANDALA

T HE PLANE SAT ON the tarmac, waiting its turn for take off. The 11-seat-across Boeing 757 was on its way to Oslo from Newark, and packed to the gunnels with passengers. Getting-to-know-your-neighbor conversations were breaking out all over the place, with boisterous shouts and upswells of good cheer. You could hear American accents in various stripes and flavors, mixed with a polite vernacular that contained the odd angular phrase or strangely placed pause from the Scandinavians who were generous enough to speak English. At one point a "tough guy" American voice rose above all the others, and you heard: "What do I want? I'll tell you want I want. I want it all! Doesn't everybody?" It was one of those moments that stops your mind. And then I thought, *No, I really don't want it all. But how fascinating! No doubt, Mr. Tough Guy and a great swatch of humanity feel differently.* So do Celeste and Terra, the heaven and earth of The Architect ZM Type. Celeste's picture is heavenly and Terra's is earthy, and they both want it all. What's more, it feels reasonable to them to want it all.

Wanting it all can also have its fateful dark side—namely, self-inflicted financial hardship. *The Book of Changes*, the 3,000-year-old great book of the Taoist sages, addresses this in its 28th hexagram, "Preponderance of the Great."[6] The "great" refers to a degree of willfulness, a degree of wanting-ness. This is apropos the material things, aesthetics, educational experiences, life experiences, and values that one feels strongly about. The 28th hexagram is not harping on vapid materialism. The issue is more subtle than that. The Architect has a vivid, detailed picture of her family's world. The danger is that The Architect may not possess all the necessary resources to actualize that detailed picture, but she willfully proceeds anyway, *sans* prioritizing.

The strain this creates can be enormous, hence *The Book of Changes* makes reference to it as "fear of collapse." This may be a bit dramatic for our purposes; nonetheless, we should carefully consider the matter. In the "Preponderance of the Great" hexagram, two images point to this theme of collapse: one from the heavens and one from the earth. The first image is the "ridgepole," that which holds up the roof of the house. The ridgepole is under great strain and might break. In ordinary times, the weight of The Architect's attachments is stressful, but she may get by. She might even get used to that stress—the financial stress of sending her kids to Waldorf or Montessori or some amazing private school, and living in the right house in the right neighborhood in the right town, and eating good organic fresh food, and you get the picture. Nothing super-crazy going on here. Though it does add up. In the end, financial vulnerability looms.

Contemplate, if you will, the second image of the hexagram, that of tsunami: (an) "extraordinary time...when water rises up above the trees." Heaven forbid that "extraordinary" times arrive for the already-stretched Architect. Great events like recession and depression and inflation impact the multitudes. These are big events outside anyone's control. Such times require flex and resourcefulness and attentiveness, the opposite of stubborn attachment or rigid idealism.

While these images of collapse are dramatic, what leads up to them is not. It is a story of the myriad details, day-in day-out, creating causes and conditions that one day karmically come home. Hemingway, in his first novel, *The Sun Also Rises*, articulates this in the clever exchange between Bill and Mike:

> *"How did you go bankrupt?"* Bill asked.
> *"Two ways,"* Mike said. *"Gradually and suddenly."*[7]

Being attached to things and experiences is rarely the vapid materialistic display that pop culture likes to flaunt. It is subtle. And by the way, attachment is not categorically bad. Thank God Mom is attached to her children and Mama Bear is attached to her cubs. That sense of good attachment extends out, and much of it is clear and intelligent: eighth-grade graduation ceremony requires a new dress, and a new dress requires new shoes, and accessories…to a point! That is, to a very sharp point, like that of a good sword.

A SWORD NAMED "P"

This (a good sword) is what The Architect must unsheath, even if she'd rather not. It is the sharp sword that cuts through, and prioritizes. It is a ruthless disciplined sword that pares away seeming must-haves, a humble sword that relegates some projects to the back burner, a sage sword that guards the projects that blossom over time, and a courageous sword that cuts through the demand, "Manifest my world NOW!"

Cutting through takes work, and willingness. Prioritizing is a pain for The Architect. Terra likes to grow people, things, flowers, food. In her way, she wants it all. Celeste likes to feast, lavishly, brilliantly, preferably like the Olympian Immortals. In her way, she too wants it all. This feels reasonable. Spring and Summer and Harvest time are eternal. That feels reasonable. Except they are not eternal! Winter happens. Glory and expansion cannot be forever. Winter has its place, and then some. It is cool and cold, and it cuts through attachment. The Architect is well equipped to wield that cool sharp sword. She can prioritize. She can cut and cut skillfully. But will she?

In this preliminary stage, Money Mandala is NOT the answer. Not yet. The Architect herself is the answer. This mature planning work is hers. Only The Architect can discern and decide and arrange and design the elements accordingly. This is her style of ruling in the land of Hearth Money. Planning-wise, this is no yin sovereign. Yang, action, cutting is called for. Of course, a "thought-partner" can support her in this process of prioritizing. Once this mature planning work is done, others (mainly Maven Types) can complement her world, via savvy implementation. Then the table is set. Then, yes, The Architect can periodically have it all. It will be right. It will be a beautiful thing.

NOTES ON MONEY MANDALA RX FOR THE ARCHITECT ZM TYPE

FIRST AND FOREMOST

Puella must go. Puella is the woman who wears the t-shirt— "Just Give Me the Fairy Tale"—and means it! Her refusal to prioritize invites distress and hardship. Can't do much with puella around. I will not belabor the point. By the by, there is nothing wrong with you, The Architect, mustering a thought-partner, to help you sort things out and prioritize. Planning is yang for you.

KEEP BIG MONEY IMPLEMENTATIONS A SOCIAL EXPERIENCE

Implementation, however, is yin. It is not for you to do in isolation. Price is what screws you up. Ignoring it doesn't work. Looking at it doesn't work. Moving through your money world without regard to what things cost, is a recipe for trouble. On the other side of the coin, when you do think price, Dear Architect, you are ineffective because you don't consistently get that either; and probably never will! Like The Creative Type, your thoughts about the price of things are erratic. Therefore, the rule is:

> The Architect does no major financial implementing by herself.

By yourself, you are forever subsidizing the rest of the world by paying full retail price for things. *OK, that seems like a decent price,* you say, but really you have no idea. While **planning** shows you as active and creating and cutting, **implementing** has you working well in the opposite mode: gathering, receiving, considering, and finally deciding. Deciding on the Audi A-6 station wagon is your strong suit; following your Maven husband's lead to buy it in Fort Collins instead of Boulder and save $125/month on the lease contract is your yin wisdom. The guy has researched the heck out of the Audi A-6 universe and he knows price. You go with that. That is implementation as social experience.

BOTTLENECKS ARE TELLTALE

Sometimes small things can have all-pervading implications. I am reminded of a dear friend, Anna, who comes from an old money family, where women received money in trust and (financially speaking) were never totally respected or empowered. An elegant, erudite woman in her early 60's, a Celeste Type, she also suffers from anxiety around her money, particularly regarding expenditure. She never really knows where she stands, in terms of what she has and what she is spending, until long after the fact.

The remedy seems simple enough: hire a bookkeeper to come in once a month for a few hours and download all the info and format it, so she can have a clear picture of what is going on.

That recommendation was made four years ago. I cannot report that anything has changed in this regard, which is unfortunate for Anna. In the meantime she pines: *I know I should be doing the Quicken stuff myself. It's my job. It would be good for me. Besides, paying someone $30/hour to do this seems silly.* These are the erratic price thoughts of The Architect. Hung up on $30/hour, hung up on $800/year, a mere pittance compared to her overall annual expenditure.

THE BETTER DEVIL

Naturally, if the bottleneck is removed and Anna receives good, clear, real-time information, she'll also be confronted with a new daunting task: to periodically unsheath the sword and cut away parts of her personal financial world that are not in line with her budget and her priorities. Anxiety from not knowing where she stands is the devil Anna knows. Anxiety from knowing and cutting is the devil Anna doesn't know. Rooted in the Voodoo City of N'Orleans, *Zen Money Blues* much prefers the latter. As for Anna, only time will tell.

FOUNDATION

Every ZM Type functions best on good information, current

and accurate. The budget is foundational. Tracking is critical. Good information informs everything, including purchases. Sometimes price trumps beauty. The budget is there to remind you that cutting is needed. Getting everything might not be an option. Prioritizing might be called for. Other times the plan, the price, the budget all come together, and you can have it all. Good to know that, too.

THE MINDFULNESS GAME

The Creative, as we will learn, has his "early warning system" practice of catching himself, letting the slightest doubt wake himself up. You, Dear Architect, have a different mind game to play:

Look, but don't believe.

Look refers to looking at the price tag. Sorry if this ruins an otherwise delightful afternoon of retail therapy. The information is important, just not to you. No sass intended here, it's just that what you think about price isn't that important (that's the "don't believe" part). What's important is that you have the information stored away in your mind for your people, your Money Mandala, which of course has a healthy representation of Mavens in it. They will want to know about price (your information) when you seek their advice. Secondarily, price is mentally registered for another reason: you have a budget, and the numbers have to add up. If, habitually, you don't have a budget and a number in mind when you shop, you're playing with fire, Dear Architect.

ENTER THE HERO

Mavens are heroes. OK, so they can be a little loud and overbearing, and occasionally tough to take. But they are the answer. The good ones shop the sales' rack like professional buyers, shop the Farmers' Market like farmers, buy furniture after myriad conversations and articles read, vacation like kings for plebe rates, build the eco-house better, manage the checkbook better, what have you. Mavens also love to share. For you—The Architect—trying to balance the budget AND shop can be an incendiary affair, a kind of Fort Sumter for personal finance. No one wishes that civil war on you.

Mavens can make the numbers of your budget work. You don't have that prowess. They do. You have the weekly menu of household meals, they tell you where to buy the ingredients for it. Or perhaps they give you information that it's time to tweak the menu based on seasonality: *It's September and Wild King Salmon is in, fresh, packed with Omega-3's, and the price is the best you're going to see all season!* Mavens are amazing this way.

Akin to The Creative's Money Mandala Rx, you are not beholden to any one Maven. Nor are all Mavens the same, in terms of taste, interest, or quality of Maven-ness. Your task, then, is to vet through the universe of Mavens, to find those who best serve your purposes. This dynamic is self-selecting anyway. If you consort with Mavens and then consistently do not take their advice, they lose interest in you, because more often than not they'll follow up with you and want to know how that restaurant was, or how that car salesman acted, and what kind of bid that contractor made.

HIRING THE MAN

Professional Mavens have their place in your Money Mandala. To them, offload as many tasks as you dare, while staying connected. This prescription is NOT exclusive to the high-falutin' Celeste. Terra and Celeste of Walden Pond will do very well by this, too. CPA's, financial planners, investment advisors, attorneys, mail/

bill-pay services, and bookkeepers are all mission-critical implementers. For The Architect, at this stage of the game, it's about getting things done, and done well, at the right price. Professionals who are skilled and conscientious and perky drive tremendous value for The Architect. These professionals are paid to be proactive and push things through to completion—to make sure the family revocable trust is not only executed, but that the assets are titled in the name of the new trust. Your job as Architect is to find these professional gems, and design relationships with them based on checks and balances, on delegating, on intelligent letting-go. (See Creative Rx for more detail on this.)

SPEAKING OF HEROES

There is a time when the hero is you, Dear Architect. There is a time when design trumps price. When design MUST trump price. Then you must prevail. Then your reputation is everything. But there are requirements. Heroes have to be worthy. Have to go through their own trials and tribulations; cultivate discipline; carefully earn the respect of others; and stow away lessons learned, so there can be no mistake in the moment of truth.

In the summer of 2004, some family friends (Smitty and Leila), were about to embark on a home remodel. Unbeknownst to me, they had followed up on my recommendation to contact Elaine, a feng shui consultant of fine pedigree. As luck would have it, I popped by during the consult, and it was easy to see that Elaine, speaking her "grand-design mind," was getting a mixed reception. Arms crossed, Smitty was not smiling. Leila, on the other hand, was taking copious notes and nodding a lot!

Smitty pulled me aside and grizzled: *Elaine wants the roof to go. Said the pitch and eaves spell trouble. Daggers, ill health, anger. I told her, That's a major change, not in the plan, expensive, not sure where I'll come up with the funds for that. She said: It's got to go—that's it!*

That afternoon Smitty was one big head-shake. Leila was one big nod. Elaine repeatedly confirmed Leila's thoughts on what worked and what did not work in the remodel plan. Much of that for Leila was an intuitive thing: she had the picture but not the words. What's more, this was truly a coincidental meeting of the minds, between Elaine and Leila, because Elaine is infamous for her blunt style, regardless of how wealthy or important her clients are.

In the end, Leila prevailed and Smitty got over it. In fact, much later he became "the converted." Living life on the other side of the remodel project (which incorporated Elaine's major changes), Smitty was wont to say: *Best money ever spent...making these changes. The energy's completely different in here. Leila is upbeat, and you know how that goes: when she's happy, I'm happy.*

Now a few folks out there might think feng shui is a fad or a cult or that it's some Asian mumbo jumbo, and maybe they're right, but the analogy for these *Zen Money Blues* purposes stands: Certain elements of The Plan, be it life or financial or architectural, must never be compromised. This is the potency and the cosmic mandate of The Architect. Health and well-being can never be sacrificed, nor diminished by price. The same goes for love—romantic, parental, filial, and so on. The same goes for work—the proverbial "room with a view" suggests greatness and inspiration every time you lift your gaze and look out at the mountains and the plains. Success begets success. People know this. Yet people forget this all the time. Design does matter. Planning does matter. Celeste knows this. Terra knows this. Celeste of Walden Pond knows this. This is the incalculable wisdom of The Architect. Not every Architect will have the luxury of tag-teaming her spouse with a feng shui master; therefore, guard your character and integrity with your life. Sometimes, the moment of truth arrives, and everyone is depending on you…and your incalculable wisdom: Then your Word is everything.

LOVE IN THE TIME OF PROSPERITY

Smitty and Leila are illustrative of what often happens in life and marriage, despite our best conscious efforts: we marry our opposite. Morning person, night person. Introvert, extravert. Thinking, feeling. Archer, Creative. Architect, Maven. *The Book of Changes* cites the seed of conflict as diverging elements.[8] Equally, it describes the peace and prosperity that come from the union of heaven and earth. Opposites can complement and generate, or diverge and destroy. The couples who can sort out financial roles and responsibilities, based on their financial identities, have the best shot at ZM Type harmonizing, of keeping money out of the bedroom. Some folks just luck into it, or intuit it. But many folks don't. Good folks. Then money becomes a virus, invading home life and marriage. That virus, of course, is contempt. So please, Dear Reader, take great care with all this. It is difficult to do the world some good if your marriage is primarily a wounding, de-energizing experience.

INVESTMENTS—PLANNING

Crafting an Investment Policy Statement with your investment or financial advisor is of the first order. Already, you know what you want and when: retirement, midlife crisis car, midlife crisis bucolic retreat, big family holiday, funds for children, grandchildren, bigger house or smaller house, senior co-housing facility, weddings, charitable gifting, etc.. You communicate the visualization. Your advisor puts the numbers to it, and considers that in light of your risk profile. Quantifying goals is a good idea. Then you have crisp numbers that clarify how much to save for tomorrow, and how much to spend now.

As ever, keep the numbers conservative. Take only as much risk as you need to take. This may be hard for you. More risk equals more return, on paper. In reality, it also means a truly lively ride through markets that could break your heart. Having "more" at retirement may sound like "more" fun, but really the task for you is to answer a different question: really, how much is enough? Identify that and stick with it. Besides, risk itself has its point of diminishing returns. This is to say, there is a point where more risk does NOT equal more return. The same is true for "alpha" (beating the markets). Few professionals consistently beat the markets.[9] History does not equivocate on these matters.

INVESTMENTS—IMPLEMENTATION

Craft that Investment Policy Statement, talk through your risk profile, communicate your plans and pictures, and come home to how much is really enough. Then engage the services of a financial professional (or truly inspired Archer spouse) who is a skilled implementer. Someone who not only knows best in class with regards to investments, but someone who works all the pieces around your money—internal investment expenses, tax efficiencies, coordination and communication with the other people (particularly, your accountant) in your mandala. Details matter. Continuity counts. Such a financial professional brings considerable benefit to all the ZM Types.

Regarding you, Dear Architect, that professional someone is also best endowed with a steadfast temperament. Someone who will not be swayed by overtures to ditch the investment plan or chase alpha. A few silver hairs do not hurt. This Seasoned Pro goes with the numbers. Is a student of history. Alpha (beating the markets) is hard to come by. Year-in year-out 80% or so of equity mutual fund managers aim to beat the market, and fail. Individual investors, putting their money with them, sometimes do even worse. This is to say, they do even worse than the returns of the underperforming funds! This is not so good. Of late, a lot of attention has been paid to this in the press. *Morningstar.com* quantified it, and put a label on it: "Return to Investors."[10] This particular metric calculates what investors actually make when investing in a given mutual fund. Easy deduction follows suit. Starting with mediocre investment funds, a good portion of these investors try to time the market and inadvertently achieve the opposite result: they buy high and sell low. We can only infer why, and in *Zen Money Blues*, we do just that, one ZM Type at a time.

Which segues back to the subject of the Seasoned Pro and you, Dear Architect. Such a grounded financial professional will be up to it when you start voicing the idea of tampering with the plan. The Seasoned Pro will be poised. Won't be intimidated by your push or pull. For him, all roads lead to home. That is, to the Investment Policy Statement. This is constitutional, and written for good reason. Why, it's one thing if the advisor is not managing your investments according to the Investment Policy Statement. It's another thing altogether, when you are feeling restless and imagining that the solution is to ditch the plan—the plan that you wrought once upon a time, when cool heads prevailed. The Seasoned Pro remembers that time, vividly so, and will assuredly bring you back to that time, too.

LISTS FOR LIST PEOPLE: THE ARCHITECT ZM TYPE

FOCUS OF FINANCIAL PLANNING FOR THE ARCHITECT TYPE:

1) First and Foremost: Never forget the sword of "P." Only you can prioritize, because you hold the whole picture.

2) Planning? This is your specialty!

3) Do you need a thought-partner to sort out your many plans? Prioritize?

4) How much is enough?

5) Establish a working budget (if you don't have one in place; also, keep it current).

6) Compose Investment Policy Statement with advisor. Properly talk through risk/reward. General rule of thumb: take on as little risk as possible to accomplish your financial goals.

FOCUS OF IMPLEMENTATION FOR THE ARCHITECT TYPE:

1) The Rule: Smile on your peculiar glitch of erratic price thoughts. No big deal. Just keep implementation in your personal finance world a social experience.

2) Gather your people = create your Mandala. Heavy on The Mavens: bookkeeper, administrative assistant, investment counselor, financial advisor, spouse, and so forth. One or two core people will suffice for most of it, though having a network of Mavens, expert in areas essential and odd, is an ongoing job for you.

3) Gather your people—encore. The plan has been fleshed out; now who exactly do you need to effectively put it into action? You may already have received instructions up the wazoo from your husband or mother-in-law. In fact, you've received "Maven transmissions" a million times over in your life: *Don't buy golf clubs through this seller on eBay; go to such and such seller.* Or, *Buy your veggies and cheeses from the Farmers' Market. The best in terms of price and quality are from Snyder's Farm...* So really examine your world, and your budget, and identify which areas could use a price and/or quality upgrade, then find The Mavens-in-waiting. They're out there.

4) Are there services (i.e., Maven services, implementation services) that make sense for you? That really represent a value proposition for you? For example, the Quicken Gal at $30/hour, or $80/month not only assuages anxiety and guilt (because budget-tracking is not getting done with the regularity that it should), but such a service upgrades the Hearth Money scene, whereby you (The Architect) receive good information and can make much savvier planning decisions. Generally speaking, my recommendation is that you have helper-implementers in your world, and make a line on your budget for these expenses: bookkeeper, car buyer, mail/bill-pay service, Maven buddies who will shop with you, et al. Some of this may seem a bit posh, and not in line with how you see yourself. But I believe the psychic-financial dividends will more than reward you. Whenever feasible, get others to implement for you. (See Creative Implementation List for more details on this.)

5) In any case, a reliable tracking system is a must. As for The Creative, the formatting of the information must speak to you. (See Creative Implementation List for more detail on these reports, too.)

6) Gather your people—thrice. The excellent financial advisor (Seasoned Pro) is a mainstay. You make the plan. You empower the advisor to manage and implement. Pick a groove for periodic review.

7) Compensate your people fairly. This is NOT the place to Mavenize or indulge erratic price thoughts. When it comes to the professional folks in your Money Mandala, seek quality for a reasonable price. No professional likes to be knocked around on price. On the other hand, if the fee seems out of line, or you just don't know what is reasonable, confer with your other Money Mandala people. If the fee is, in fact, out of line, then move on. There is a whole universe of professionals with excellence, integrity, experience, and a reasonable fee schedule. The short of it is: never let compensation become a splinter in the relationship between you and any member of your trusted Money Mandala. You're counting on them.

8) Take stock of bottlenecks in your personal financial world. Look at them as a call-to-action. This is a riff from before, with a more mundane twist. The reason is, from time to time, I have come across obvious Architect Types, who have clear organized pictures of their financial world, and yet their home office is a quagmire of papers. Therefore, add to the list of possible helpers: an office organizer. I know this sounds really anal, but it could save your financial life.

9) Bless your Money Mandala. Your people are there for you. You've chosen them. If someone's not working out, then make the change. Sovereignty for you is dynamic: yang (active) planner, yin (receptive) implementer. Know your mind. Empower others to implement.

Chapter 15

THE MAVEN'S
MONEY MANDALA

OO OFTEN, MAVEN MATH is this: the whole equals less than the sum of the parts. This is not good. The pages of the Wall Street Journal display a never-ending stream of articles about sundry investors who want to break up a targeted company. There is logic to this. The pieces of the company, if broken apart and standing alone, are worth substantially more than the current value of the whole company kept together. The marketplace is very smart. It attacks inefficiencies. It sees that each piece is solid and valuable. May have been purchased for a very smart price. At the same time, the marketplace sees that the pieces don't all fit together. There is no unifying binding factor. No overarching vision. The architecture, if you will, is weak. Hence, the value of the conglomerate often suffers. It tries to diversify its holdings, acquire various companies, but in the end, people say: *I don't get it.*

For The Maven ZM Type, the personal financial equivalent of this is: *We have Vanguard investments and a time share in Costa Rica and flipped a couple of properties and we get killer deals wherever we go, but it doesn't add up: for some reason what we have falls short of what we should have. I don't get it.* While The Maven has special knowledge and skilled methods and zeal-for-the-deal like no other, The Maven needs a cohesive vision. He will need to put a value on the "soft side" of financial life: relationships, trust, loyalty, perspective, humility, and yes, architecture. He might even need to pay for that vision. This may chafe him. But those soft side elements cannot be overlooked. Cohesive vision transforms Maven math. Indeed, it is difficult to accomplish your goals when the whole equals less than the sum of the parts.

THE MAVEN WE LOVE

Time and again, The Maven is lovable and fun. At a party he hears you're thinking about taking up cycling and he is all over you: *I love telling other people how to spend their money!* You tell him how much you're willing to spend, and next thing you know there are cycling magazines at your house, and then you're over at his house visiting the dozen bicycles affixed upside down to the rafters of his garage. He's already thought about the right person for you to approach at University Bicycles, when that fellow works, where you pay full price (*that would be for the bike itself*) and where you push for "the deal" (*that would be on the accessories, of course: because cycling is all about the accessories...*). It might even become a bit of sensory and data overload when he insists that you try out all six "different" bikes that he has that are just like the one he's thinking you should buy. *I mean, you have to try them first. See how each one feels. No other way to know.*

The Maven is a nut, and his enthusiasm is infectious, and generally what he puts you through is a world-class due diligence process. There are myriad "lite" versions of The Maven-in-Action that bring a smile to the face. You follow him through rain and snow to get to the hole-in-the-wall Italian restaurant in Little Italy, with the red and white checked table cloths and the table wine that tastes biblical, and you talk loudly and eat and point with your fork like everyone else, and then the bill comes and it's delightfully ridiculous: you've had this great fulsome experience for a song! Those are the moments of Maven Immortality. For that he is eternally beloved.

DARK MAVEN—THE RAVEN MAVEN

Cynic was Oscar Wilde's word for he "who knows the price of everything and the value of nothing." The Raven Maven is Wilde's cynic personified. To begin with, Mavens are transaction-oriented, moving through a universe of commodities: cars, groceries, houses, travel, and the like. The internet has vastly increased the menu of the universe of commodities and information on commodities. It used to be that you needed a travel agent to implement travel plans, or a stockbroker to buy stock. That service was nice and all, maybe even more convenient, but the actual value of the service was modest. The rise of the web is accompanied by the rise in the prowess of The Maven. This is good.

But then it can go too far.

More than a few businesses have tried to commoditize relationships. Case in point: Dell Computer "outsourced" (code word for "commoditized") its customer service call centers to India earlier in the decade, because the world is "flat"[11] (i.e., connected by the web and broadband); and in the process, Dell darn near lost half its corporate customers, so bad was the service and so furious were the customers. Dell simply did not want to pay for people to manage relationships. This attempt to commoditize relationship was a cynical and costly move for Dell. The Raven Maven has the same issue.

Relationship is what The Maven sorely needs in order to counterbalance his lack of planner acuity, but it is relationship that The

Raven Maven repels. Repels by devaluing relationship. The Maven wants a deal, even on services provided by others. Sometimes this may be appropriate. Often times it's not. The Maven doesn't want to pay full price. Implicit in that is the expectation that others—people—will not deliver. Earlier in *Zen Money Blues* we discussed this reality. Relationships are messy. Some people deliver what they say they will, and some don't. That variation in quality delivered is vexing. Nor can it be 100% controlled, and, well, it's kind of obvious, The Maven likes control and likes his predictable outcomes. But being cynical does not help the matter.

The Maven, however, is not destined to be cynical. This is not a matter of wiring. Raven Mavens can change. Cynicism is an adopted, cultivated outlook and mode of behavior. What's more, devaluing relationship "works" for some people. This is true. There are strange payoffs involved, including the squeaky-wheel-gets-the-oil syndrome. Modern Analysts and their kin could, I'm sure, fully explain the whys and wherefores of this. That's all beyond me. But the bottom line remains: Being cynical is a choice. The Maven can decide whether to care for the relationships in his Hearth Money world, starting with the full contact Yard Sailors and extending out to his bookkeeper, gardener, mechanic, acupuncturist, financial planner, accountant, and family attorney.

Care doesn't mean The Maven needs to become a puddle that the other guy walks through and splashes about. Care means he respects the human elements at play. Quality professionals aren't just in it for the money. In fact, if Richard Florida's book, *The Creative Class*,[12] is any indication, compensation is typically NOT the number one reason a broad spectrum of Americans do the work they do. Meaning is a fundamental element—a core value. Quality professionals and business people are not looking for annoying client relationships. Even if the pay is excellent, the psychic cost is not worth it. They're looking for meaningful, gratifying relationships, that pay decently-to-very-well.

It is just such high quality, high integrity people who complement The Maven's gifts. Who bring him back into balance, who provide him with valuable perspective, who make sure that Maven math is undone—that the whole is no longer less than the sum of the parts. On the balance sheet of many corporate financial statements, there is an asset line for "Good Will." Good will has value, sometimes significantly so. Good will is the company's good name. Good will is the value in the marketplace of the subjective elements—the good feelings and confidence that that brand or company engenders in its customers. Apple (the company) is iconic in this regard. Its customers are a cult consumer nation, loyal and engaged. Good will is no abstraction for them, and the benefits are huge. Commoditizing relationships, unfortunately, goes in the opposite direction. It puts no value on good will. There is no consideration given to the long view, to how things shake out over time. Most quality professionals want quality long-term relationships with the individuals and families they work with. Cynics go in the opposite direction. They end up more often than not working with cynical professionals, who take a short-term opportunistic view of things themselves. Talk about the irony of the self-selecting and self-fulfilling universe! Non-relationship folks working with non-relationship folks: hmm, I wonder how that ends!

Notes on Money Mandala Rx for The Maven ZM Type

First and Foremost

Remember the classic children's book by Maurice Sendak, *Pierre*.[13] The parents go through crazy humorous interactions with young Pierre (*I'll let you fold the folding chair!* his father pleads, to which young Pierre says, *I don't care*). The parents are desperate for Pierre—insouciant at the age of 7!—to say that he cares. They try and they try, to no avail. The story culminates with the parents leaving him home alone, at which time an opportunistic lion appears. The lion engages the boy on a number of matters, and Pierre, of course, continues his indifferent ways. *I don't care*. Finally, the lion says, *Then I'll eat you up*, and Pierre on cue says, *I don't care*. So the lion eats him! I myself found that part of the story very satisfying. But not to worry. The story doesn't end there. This is no Brothers Grimm ending. The parents come home and bash the lion over the head and turn him upside down and shake him, and out of his mouth pops Pierre, who this time screams, *I care, I care!*

Dear Maven, your Money Mandala cannot possibly work right until you care about your people. You don't have to hug a tree together, or anything like that. Just honor that they have a lot to offer you, to really support and super-charge your powerful Maven activities. Value them. Pay them properly.

In a word, Care.

WITH A LITTLE HELP FROM YOUR FRIENDS

Getting the right people in your Money Mandala is no solo heroic task. It is an architectural issue, and it is a people issue. Planning is best a social experience for you. Seek assistance. Any of the other three ZM Types can certainly help you in identifying quality folks—who do what they do for a fair rate. Do not automatically discard the recommendation from a Creative Type: he knows relationship better than all. But probably The Archer will be your most trusted advisor. In any case, begin at the heart-center. You need a financial planner. Find her, whether she be spouse or professional or great family friend. With her, it should be easy to design your Money Mandala and ascertain who the relevant players are. This is planning. Planning is best a social experience for you.

KEEP PLANNING A SOCIAL EXPERIENCE

You are yang master in the realm of implementation. Planning, however, is different. Requires other people, a modicum of stillness, and forethought. Ascertaining the right targets for you is not some simple formula. It comes of human relationship, and dialogue, and considerable contemplation. You should know your mission, Heroic Maven, before you embark. Always. Jetting off in search of the next great deal, *sans* plan, is contraindicated. It might be fun sport, which could be fine, as long as everyone (including yourself) is not counting on you. Therefore, the rule is:

The Maven requires plans and priorities, carefully wrought through his relationship with planner sorts. No solo planning or prioritizing indicated.

The people of your Money Mandala will bring you home to your values. Will get you to stop and think and declare. What's important to you informs your whole Hearth Money world. What's important to you is really a matter of life and death. No drama intended here. All the time people get sidetracked by things they later deem unimportant; sidetracked for days and weeks and sometimes years on end; and then they expire. That "Life happens while you're making plans" stuff just ain't true for you. That might be your reason to eschew planning, but it won't work. Coming home to yourself is what matters most. Then everything you do will add up. Then you can plunge into the timelessness of the moment, Mavenize in heroic fashion, and this will be right and true.

Sasha's Return On Time

"Price myopia" is symptomatic of a bigger planning deficit: not having your priorities straight. It is the pursuit of Maven activity at all costs, even when your "return on time" is abysmal. The following I would say is a bit of an exaggeration, except that I have heard this story with mine own ears.

Sasha is a bright, cheerful young lady, who loves a deal. Her parents are coming to town for a visit, and that reminds her that it's time for new linens, and her Maven-ness kicks in. Between and amid her morning errand routine, she goes to Marshalls, Target, and Bed, Bath & Beyond. For Sasha tells herself, *Just going and buying the linens at any old store is a fool's approach.* She peruses the goods, and knows which linens are too cheap, just one thread away from a good snag that frays and ruins them, so she establishes right quality. Now it's a matter of price—best price for that quality. She circles back for one more thorough look at price, while making sure that quality is like-kind, since the brands are not the same at the different stores. Then she makes it so. She accomplishes Mavenhood once again.

But at what price? Caught in the timelessness of pursuing best-in-linens, Sasha spent precious hours driving round town, to save what, a few bucks? How efficient was that? What in fact was the return on her time (not to mention price of gas, CO_2 emitted, and so on)? In economic terms, the question is one of opportunity cost. While she was spending hours implementing her linens task, what else was she not doing? Not earning? Not billing for? Not tending to, that now require paying someone else to take care of?

When is it better to simply get a pretty good deal that takes no time at all? When is it better to simply get those good linens, pretty good price, in and out, and on to the next thing on the list? This myopia is debilitating. The Maven gets addicted to being expert, obsesses about getting the best deal, and ignores when to let it go. Overlooks when "good enough" is sane and good and fine. Is susceptible to this like no other ZM Type.

Sasha Redux—Priorities and Values

Interestingly, the "planning antidote" isn't purely a financial equation for you, The Maven. It's not just, What are your financial planning priorities? It's much bigger. What are your life priorities? Life is short. Time is finite. How often are you cruising around in Maven mode when, after catching a moment to reflect, you have really lost control of time itself?

Thus planning is not just financial for you. It is bigger. It needs to be lined up with your values and your life's priorities, of which personal money is but one part. Sometimes in life we become attached to doing what we're really good at, irrespective of the bigger picture. Why this is so, is understandable. We all want to shine our light. However, by habitually clinging to what we're really good at, we can lose perspective. Our actions can fall out of alignment with the bigger picture, and thus become counterproductive. Dear Maven, plan well your movements before you make them. You have tremendous power and skill and energy. Make sure that it is not all for less. Hitting the right targets is mission-critical. Don't leave that to chance. Don't be hopeful. Know in advance what the right targets are. For that, rely on your people. Speak your mind and gather their counsel and ponder it all. You will be well served by such a pre-Maven routine.

MATCH MADE IN HEAVEN

You have so much to gain from harmonizing with The Architect, be that in the form of a spouse or friend, or someone who does this professionally. When you, Heroic Maven, have someone in your world who periodically prompts you to think about what the objectives are and why they are the objectives; when you have someone who can carry the "institutional" memory of the family regarding goals and implementation plans, thereby creating a sense of continuity to yours and everyone's activity; when you have someone who can give you a job, a clear task to be implemented— then you are free and potent and cannot miss. Success is assured.

JERRY'S DEAD, PHISH SUCKS, GET A JOB

It must have been the late 90's and I saw someone walking around the Pearl Street mall with this on his t-shirt and it cracked me up. That being said, I am sorry Jerry is dead, I don't think Phish's intellectual iconoclastic music sucks, but "Get a Job" perfectly serves our purposes here. You, The Maven, need a job. Lots of 'em. You are wired to work, and work well. On the personal finance homefront, the management of checkbook and allowance dispensing and budget-tracking and implementation of purchases large and small should go to you. The heavy lifting is for you to do. This is good.

LOVE IN THE TIME OF PROSPERITY—PART II

Disdain not, Dear Maven. No one can implement like you— no one. Chances are very good that your spouse or significant other is not a Maven like you. So, go easy. The Creative and The Architect you may feel Darwinian disdain for; and their blind-spots may indeed doom them to personal financial extinction; but go easy. Be kind to others, especially those closest to you.

Everyone has something to work on in the Zen Money universe. Everyone.

There may be a time when your wife wants to find a horse for her daughter, and there is a lot going on. You know I'm not talking about the money. Your wife has a picture of the process she wishes to go through, to find the horse that is just right for her (and your) daughter. When you opened your mouth to tell your wife how to get the best deal, she politely told you to buzz off. It's important, really important, emotionally important—this finding the right horse ritual. It is suffused with your wife's stories from yesteryear, and the initiation of your daughter to young-woman-hood today.

In the end it may cost the family 4K more to do it your wife's way, and that's OK. I know you hate leaving 4K on the table. But then something altogether different would have transpired, such that the shared journey of acquiring a horse probably would have gone away, meaning a great opportunity lost. You heard the words of your planner: that 4K is not going to make or break your situation. Therefore, let it be.

And you did.

It was hard and you did. Your wife had genuine wisdom at play, and your Maven DNA was screaming inside, and you got to the other side. You let it be. Yes, your wife is The Creative Type. In unconscious mode, she is at risk of being the painful perfect opposite of the cynic; so dubbed, The Wise Fool, who "knows the value of everything and the price of nothing." But she is not the unconscious Creative. The Money Mandala is working. No harm is coming to you or your family. 4K, I must add, is a small price to pay for Mother and Daughter to come together, to have a meeting of hearts and minds about coming of age. That will never happen again. Ever.

And you let it be.

INVESTMENTS—PLANNING

Craft that Investment Policy Statement with your financial advisor. As you know by now, planning is best a social experience for you. Your people are there to engage you, to prompt you with sundry questions, to organize all into a cohesive vision that includes retirement, holiday, big purchases, college funding, weddings, and so on. You may believe that you already know what that number is, say, to hit retirement, and you may be right. But go with the dialogue. It's a good one for everyone. Maybe your numbers and your advisor's numbers concur. Then there is a time line for your goals, and there is your risk profile. Now reaching your goals can truly be quantified. It is in a risk-adjusted universe, aimed at hitting clearly defined targets in specific amounts of time.

Too often has The Maven said to a would-be advisor: *Here's* _____ *amount of money. What can you do with it? How much return can you get me?* That is a setup for failure. The cliché of the financial advisory business is unequivocally true: Getting our clients to accomplish their goals is our number one job. If we take less risk and grow a client's funds slowly and steadily, and they reach their goal, then that is a job well done. The foundational planning work, in this instance, may reveal that a 9% compounding return over the next 10 years will make the client's dreams a cheerful reality. A 9% compounding return over time, we might add, is quite respectable. 80 years of market activity corroborate that view. But you, Dear Maven, are prone to chafe. To believe that, *Surely, there is someone who can do more and therefore achieve much better returns.*

It doesn't matter that you may not need better returns. It's your ethic. You want your money working hard, harder, hardest! That message comes through loud and clear. Paradoxically, the harder you work "passive investments" (and stocks and bonds are passive investments, by definition, because neither you nor I is running any of these companies), the more you increase trading costs and management fees and tax liabilities and bookkeeping costs, all of which chip away at your total return. It's called market timing and active management, and the numbers generally say that you (or any professional) only have a remote chance of "beating the market" anyway. I know it's an affront to your Maven ways, but the numbers speak for themselves.

Should you apprentice properly and then set up shop to trade professionally, then perhaps you will be one of those great rebel success stories. Should you run one of these public companies, then I have no doubt you could drive tremendous return on equity. However, both examples are about Hunter Money. Hunting. Actively working the operations of a business. Actively working investing as a business. This is another country, with its own laws and norms. Expectations for Hunter Money return on investment don't fit for Hearth Money investments. It won't work. It doesn't fit. Apples and oranges. Besides, we're talking about that part of your wealth that is not meant to be another J-O-B for you!

INVESTMENTS—IMPLEMENTATION I

Dear Maven, you are at risk of making what in my business is labeled "the worst mistake of all"—chasing returns. Earlier I referenced the Morningstar metric of "Return To Investor." Check that out. It's OK if you find it mildly disconcerting. It's the story of chasing returns—chasing last year's winners in the marketplace. Occasionally this makes sense, but not simply because you want the returns that such and such a fund or sector delivered last year.

Rather, it occasionally makes sense when you are tuning in to a much larger trend in the world markets, and that trend has a considerable ways to go.

Energy, for example, fits that bill. It will be the economic riddle that all of us, and our children, and their children will have to solve. The economics of the situation are basic: increasing worldwide demand for energy and commodities, that demand intensifying with the increase in prosperity of heavily populated emerging countries, and all of that juxtaposed with a planet of finite natural resources. Technology is a major unknown. Will we or won't we develop the next great thing that saves the day? That's not a given at all. In light of this backdrop, then yes, indeed, for the right price, it may make sense to "buy energy," which coincidentally was one of last year's winners. But most of the time, this simply is not what transpires. Wanting returns like last year's, we end up chasing old news.

You, Dear Maven, are prone to making this error because you're impatient. Long-term investing feels weak. But it is anything but weak. The numbers of the last 80 years speak volumes. Slow and steady (and diversified) wins the race. But you may also feel that this sort of investing is abstract, and in a way you're right. It is impersonal and dispassionate, looking for regressions from the historical mean and long-term corporate earnings growth. For you then, there is a natural remedy. Take a modest portion of your Hearth Money investment fund and work it as you wish. Real estate, short-term buys and sells of cars, collectibles, even stocks or currencies. Advisors call this "Crazy Money." Done prudently, even a nasty outcome won't dramatically alter your ability to accomplish your goals. But if you truly are in that 20% of professional fund managers who ultimately beat the heck out of the market, and do it year after year, then hats off to you, and enjoy the icing on the cake.

INVESTMENTS—IMPLEMENTATION II

Trust your people. Don't undercut the plan because one day you wake up and decide that you really hate 9% compounding return. Every investor-dog has his day. Value investors have had their way the past 6 years. Growth investors ruled before that, for much of the 90's. Beating the markets (alpha) is tough. There are a lot of smart chaps and chappiettes who work in the investment management world and can't beat the markets. Instead, focus on the things that you and your advisor can control: internal expenses, taxes, superior asset class diversification, and managing risk. Just don't kill the plan.

DOES THE MAVEN CATCH A BAD RAP?

You may be familiar with the recent United States Supreme Court ruling on The Maven...well, maybe not. But the rap on you, Dear Maven, is this: you're stubborn and hands-down the least advisor-receptive of all the ZM Types. Perhaps Maven Nation is in need of hiring a publicity agency, thereby garnering the requisite amount of spin. Perhaps. But beyond all of this fantasy fun, I'd like to really encourage you to engage in a meaningful relationship with a planner sort. Cutting corners can be funky. I am reminded of a phrase I used to hear back in the day, when mountain climbing was a religion in my life: *There are no shortcuts in the high country.* Truer words have not been spoken. In the high country, shortcuts will get you killed. The map is the map. The routes are the routes. Folks who blaze new trails in the high country rarely end up heroes. Sticking to the map, sticking to the trails, actually makes a lot of sense. There's nothing wrong with being a hero, just not with personal money. There's nothing wrong with being a hero, as long as you have medical insurance, and life insurance, and perhaps disability insurance, just in case things don't work out as you imagined they would. The planner kind of person is your natural guide. Will you follow?

LISTS FOR LIST PEOPLE: THE MAVEN ZM TYPE

FOCUS OF FINANCIAL PLANNING FOR THE MAVEN TYPE

1) Engage the cool perspective and wisdom of the planner: someone who can help establish the vision; someone who can provide continuity of focus over time (i.e., "hold the vision," "retain family financial memory"). Remember: Vision leads, Maven (implementer) follows.

2) Some relationships are worth it. You need people. You need counsel. Loosen the control thing. You need help sorting out the various items you want to accomplish. You need lists. You need counterbalance. Raven Maven hell—it's not a fun place to end up in.

3) Price isn't everything—Part I. Sometimes the best deal isn't really the best deal, such as when your plane flight from Denver to New York has two stops and you're waylaid in Detroit on a winter's night. Poor planning and obsessive implementing waste time, and time—you no doubt recognize—is a precious commodity, too.

4) As it is for The Creative, so it is for The Maven: the planning piece need not be every day. After some initial work, a once or twice a year "check in" should more than suffice, unless of course there is a sudden major decision (e.g., purchase, investment, etc.) on the docket. In the area of investments, you might follow the lead of your investment advisor regarding which risk/reward universe to place your investments in. Then, if you have interest in stocks, bonds, real estate, it may well behoove you to find a slice of the pie for you to engage and "work your money."

5) Price isn't everything—Part II. Good counsel, be it from accountants, lawyers, or advisors, costs money. Sometimes this goes in the "best money ever spent" category.

6) Loyal, trustworthy "thought-partners" never hurt. Know the rules for transaction; know the rules for relationship.

7) Value your Money Mandala people. They're there for you. You've chosen them. If someone's not working, then make the change. Sovereignty for you is dynamic: yin (receptive) planner, yang (active) implementer.

8) Above all, take the time to know what is most important to you.

FOCUS OF IMPLEMENTATION FOR THE MAVEN TYPE

1) You're a Maven. You own implementing. You love being generous with others regarding your special knowledge. This makes you beloved. This makes you a hero.

2) You are wired to do the heavy lifting: checkbooks, Quicken, Maven research, transactions large and small. Carry as much as you can. Carry it all!

3) Keep your Maven-ness learning and growing. Good information is oxygen for you.

4) Be in touch with Maven Nation. Other good Mavens keep you sharp. Like the great masters of yesterday and today, ever remain a student of the game.

Chapter 16

THE CREATIVE'S MONEY MANDALA

THE Rx FOR THE CREATIVE in managing Hearth Money is straightforward: surround yourself with excellent people, empower them, observe them, see what they're good at, and go with that. Mandala = people. Let your people prompt you. Let them lead with their relevant strengths. You follow, with intelligence and groove. Following is no slight to you. Paradoxically, this is how you rule your personal financial world. They manage your situation, while you manage them! They focus on the specific parts of your personal financial world, and you focus on them. With kindness and clarity. In the mythic-village-meets-modern-world scenario, you are akin to the "yin" sovereign—the receptive (as opposed to active) sovereign. In *The Book of Changes*, this yin sovereign is referred to in the 14th hexagram, "Possession In Great Measure," where The Judgment states:

Strength and clarity unite... How is it possible that the weak line [the yin sovereign] has power to hold the strong lines fast and to possess them? It is done by virtue of unselfish modesty. The time is favorable—a time of strength within, clarity and culture without. Power is expressing itself in a graceful and controlled way. This brings supreme success and wealth.[14]

The Creative is poised to master the situation (Hearth Money, in this case). Strength is within. He rides the energy of his inner discipline. Clarity has to do with looking out at the world—at his ministers, advisors, helpers. The Creative is receptive, AND The Creative is the decision-maker. There is no contradiction in this. Regarding personal finance, The Creative refrains from creating by himself. No planning. No implementation. Instead, he engages his people and he receives counsel and he weighs the merits and sets plans in motion. His Hearth Money world is circuitous. It is a process—a circuit, if you will, beginning with himself and running through his people back to him.

Mandala = people. The yin sovereign thus requires excellent people. They are: competent, trustworthy, and proactive. The creative holds them fast. Excellent people are strong and able. He is up to that. His natural intelligence is relationship itself. He activates that. Is assiduous. Is modest in the right way. Gathers their counsel. Is discerning on the people level. He is naturally clear here. Never lets go on this level. The yin sovereign is receptive, with intelligence. Then he will know what is worthy and what to discard. Whom to keep and whom to let go. Then The Creative can go and live his life fully.

Notes on Money Mandala Rx
for The Creative ZM Type

First and Foremost

This is not an AA meeting, I promise. But nothing can go forward until you, The Creative, make the first shift, becoming the Awake Creative and shedding (perhaps the word ought to be shredding) the Arrogant Creative. This means looking unflinchingly at the truth of your financial self, and saying out loud: *Yes, I am The Creative Type.* If you are The Creative and everyone around you knows it, and you don't want to be The Creative or are in deepest denial about it, then, well, kindly pass the salt, and after supper I had best be on my way.

The "First and Foremost" in sum is this: be who you are. If you are The Creative, embrace that. If you are the yin sovereign, go with that natural energy. Manage it. Unorthodox as it is, this approach is actually pretty cool.

KEEP BIG MONEY DECISIONS A SOCIAL EXPERIENCE

Per se, no one likes rules. But they have a governing function. Even the Hearth Money realm requires a few laws of the land, for the sake of harmony and prosperity. In this case, you, the yin sovereign, have a social contract with your people—spouse or parents, advisors or trustees, and at some point perhaps your children. The contract starts here:

> The Creative makes no major personal
> financial decisions by himself.

It is important that the distinction between major and minor decisions be manifestly clear. "Major decisions" is relative to your wherewithal. Deciding on drip coffee or latte at the café, with its dollar fifty differential, probably isn't going to set your financial house on fire. Buying a car, big toy, new home, investing in private school education, etc.—look, if it isn't clear to you where the line is, then talk it over with your spouse, significant other, advisor. Always. As often as you need.

I want to be careful here not to insult. On the other hand, I want to be careful not to gloss over your perceptions of personal financial matters, which can be seriously distorted or unrealistic, even after you are awake to your ZM Type. For example, you tend to underestimate what it takes to accomplish certain goals, and often undershoot what it actually costs to do things. Wiring is wiring. What may seem like small decisions can prove to be anything but! In planning, as with "the deal," the devil can be in the details: skipping COBRA coverage to save a few bucks between jobs; living in Colorado or Maine or Vermont and, come winter, not spending the extra 600 bucks on a set of studded tires; foregoing that gym membership as you approach the fifty-something heart attack zone; sleeping on a sunken mattress and wondering why you keep missing work and can't get enough of the chiropractor. You get the drift. The list goes on.

There's no desire here to make you paranoid, Dear Creative (nor make paranoid those who live with you and love you). Rather, just to acknowledge that regarding your personal money, you move on an intuitive/feeling or, perhaps most accurately, a non-thought level. It doesn't matter if you are an intellectual from Yale, a computer geek, or a manager of a "quant" hedge fund. When it comes to Hearth Money, your brand of logic is very difficult to trace, but probably is some cocktail of heart and emotions and sense-pleasure mixed together, dressed in the ostensible language of rationality. The progression of your mental activity is hard to capture with linear descriptors. The helter-skelter results of your activity, however, are not.

GUIDELINE—THE EARLY WARNING SYSTEM

At this point in the *Zen Money Journey*, I hope you'll grant me license to speak plainly. In your personal financial world, Dear

Creative, you have glitches. No heavy judgment here. It just is. Now that said, you may recall that a few moments ago, I noted: It is important that the distinction between major and minor decisions be manifestly clear. "Major decisions" is relative to your wherewithal. But that was a hasty oversight on my part. I assumed you know your wherewithal! You, Dear Creative, may overspend, not out of some materialistic penchant, but because—in the moment of truth, that critical moment of decision—you really have no idea where you stand financially. Things are murky. The moment is there, immediate, like a child pressing his nose against the shop window, and you say, *Yes, let's go for it. I'm "probably" financially cool anyway.*

Beware that "probably." Your people, the agents of your mandala, just aren't going to go headlong into supporting a major decision until they have been top to bottom thorough in their due diligence, and naturally that includes your wherewithal. But they can't help if you yourself plunge into it without connecting with them.

Thus arrives the early warning system guideline, for you, Dear Creative, to catch yourself before you take action and commit funds in a given direction:

> If you don't know where you stand financially and you have even one sliver of a thought that perhaps you should know before you pull the trigger on a financial decision, then treat it as if it were a "major decision."

That flicker of doubt is an ally, plain and simple. Let it stop you. Let it push you back to your mandala of people. Let it push you back to the discipline of being the yin sovereign. Personal money is best a social experience for you.

Foundation Is Good

Planning in *Zen Money Blues* connotes good planning. Competent planning. Comprehensive planning. The Architect knows how to do this, The Archer knows how to do this, and of course some of the members of your Money Mandala know how to do this by profession. The operative word here is comprehensive. Somehow, somewhere, sometime—preferably as soon as possible—you, as The Awake Creative, are required to engage and help lay down the foundation of comprehensive planning. To that table you, smile on face, bring the brown bag of unopened mail, (or perhaps the opposite, a lively assortment of folders) teeming with data on assets and liabilities, income and expenses, trust docs, wills, life insurance, health insurance. Once there, you go further. You are responsive to questions about the qualitative side, namely, your hopes and dreams, goals and objectives, fears and concerns, risk and reward, all framed in the lines of time. Foundation is laid. It is a good foundation. This is required activity. This is good.

Personal financial planning is something that need not be done every day. Naturally, if matters have fallen into disrepair, it will take a vigorous amount of energy to set things right. Fair enough. But then, once your affairs have been put in order, your goals have been laid out, and your current picture is transparent, it is a matter of upkeep and monitoring. That's where finding your groove is key.

Find Your Groove—Upkeep and Monitoring

The financial planning foundation is ordinary and solid, like a swinging unrelenting bass-line. You listen to some cool music and perhaps you don't focus in on the proverbial "bottom line," the bass-line, but your body and soul move to it anyway. On a subconscious level, it moves you. It's steady and you respond.

Doesn't have to be a big deal. The bass player is rarely going to step into the limelight, and that's all right. So it is for you, The Creative: your personal money world can be just like this.

The groove of your personal money doesn't have to change tempo all the time. It doesn't have to come into the limelight, and be a big statement or a big distraction. The bass player tends to his groove. Is committed to his groove. Rhythm is rhyme in motion. Rhythm is repetition in time, albeit with a little spice and character. Regarding personal money, *Zen Money Blues* wishes the identical ZM gig for The Creative. Tend to your groove. Tend to your money through tending to your Money Mandala relationships. Be steady.

Once the personal financial planning foundation is laid, you pick a calendar groove—say, every six months—and stick with it. This is for essential upkeep and monitoring. Planning is no one shot deal. Therefore, find what works for you and your people, and commit to it. If meeting with your Money Mandala once every six months is not enough (or too much) to keep things flowing, then so be it. Make the adjustment. Then commit to it... for a nice long time.

THE CONTRACT OF LETTING GO (THE FINE PRINT)

Let's imagine that, after contemplation and ZM test taking, you buy into the program (and it is a program, this Money Mandala Rx). You follow the rules and the guidelines, muster that early warning awareness, and commit to a groove of upkeep and monitoring. I know this might be feeling like a bit of a 12 Step Program, and maybe it is. Too soon to tell. What is clear is that you're being asked to work a big part of your life in a whole new way, and at first it may feel disagreeable. Therefore, a small discussion of the benefits (arguably, a pep talk) may be timely.

Even sovereigns need encouragement from time to time. Here goes:

Your job, more than that of any of the other ZM Types, is to learn to let go, and let go a lot. Let go all the time. But not just any kind of letting go will do. No sloppy letting go. No *Oh, what the heck, let's just do it and face the consequences later!* Nothing so devil-may-care, I'm afraid. More, it's letting go in sepias and blues. Letting go of being a free agent. Letting go of passionate plans. Letting go of a lot of what you think and feel and do about personal money. It has to be intelligent, deserved letting go.

You, The Creative, are to carry the lightest of the Hearth Money loads, but yours must be the right light load! Do that, do the Rx of Money Mandala, and you are free to not think about money much at all. Best to just let it go. During the time between meetings with your people, let the personal money ponderings go. Let the plans go. It's not yours to carry. Not your time to worry. Get your weekly cash allowance and the green light for spending within budget (you know, clothes and groceries and small stuff), and let go of the rest.

It goes further. You are hereby liberated from the day-to-day chores and periodic heavy lifting of personal finance, at least as much as you can offload. No balancing the checkbook. No paying the bills. No clipping coupons. No going toe-to-toe with the car salesman. No making the big electronics purchase by your lonesome. Not for you. Get your people involved, wherever and whenever possible.

The short version is this: personal money is not your problem. As long as you abide by the groove. As long as you don't neglect the groove.

EARTH TO MOON, OVER—

There are limitations on this theme of letting go, no doubt. Your neighbor is not suddenly going to do the grocery shopping for you. If only! But a variation of this still works: get a dang list made before you go. Get someone to help make the dang list. In one family I know, the 14 year-old daughter makes the lists before they embark on the grocery shop, and has been doing so for 8 years! Yes, she is The Architect ZM Type, and has always loved making lists and plans. Apply a similar method at Nordstrom or wherever you shop for clothes. When the sales gal says: *Can I help you with anything?* The answer is: *Yes!* If said sales gal starts laying a trip on you or gives you advice that seems insincere, then ditch her for someone else or move on to the next store. But don't go it alone. Shop with your girlfriend, guy friend, mother, you know what I mean. New clothes are nice, but outfits are much better. Letting go on this level is letting go of the illusion that you need to figure all this stuff out. This is the planning element.

MOON TO EARTH, OVER—

Implementation is seeing things through, first, and getting the good stuff at the right price, second. Don't space out on submitting the COBRA health insurance paperwork on time. Get help. Empower someone to help you see it through. Put a stop to the tendency to freewheel in isolation. Delegate!

The Saint of Personal Finance (a relation of Miss Herald's, by the by) has these reassuring words for you: *Dear Creative Type— The world wants to help you.* This I know: Mavens for sure want to help you, and possibly an Archer or two. But it's back on you. This is in your "light load." It's up to you to activate the world. Time to buy a car: huddle with the planner in your Money Mandala to find out how much you can spend, and then seek out the car

Maven. This is America, where Maven Type car-lovers abound. These fellers are just hanging around, fixing the part in their hair, waiting for an heroic Maven mission to hit their inbox. Make their day, dude. Because they'll make your day. They'll tell you dealer, make, model, lease or buy, best financing deals, whom to work with at the dealership; and they'll do it for the love. It's free.

Letting go is: tending to your part and then totally relaxing. It's like yoga: exert and relax at the same time. Exert and relax in the world. Once you've engaged the planner of your Mandala and the ad hoc inspired Maven, and everything is focused—then go for it, and enjoy. Spend your money and spend it cheerfully. Life is not just about saving. But when you save, that should be cheerful, too.

THE LIGHT LOAD

Letting go has requirements. One conspicuous element not mentioned thus far is the budget. Make a budget with your people. Don't procrastinate. It's so basic it can feel ridiculous. But it's foundational. Of the first order. Have you ever watched a builder build a house without an architect's plans? I have. The client and he were cutting corners, working off a blueprint of another house in the neighborhood that he had built, that looked "kind of the same." It was a joke, a terrible waste. So it is, proceeding in the world of Hearth Money without a budget. People do stuff like that all the time. Not a good idea.

Engage in the budgeting process, Dear Creative. Ground that budget in historical numbers. Someone else can do the down-loading and formatting in Quicken or another personal money tracker. Work off those historical numbers. That will keep it real.

Include an annual or semiannual revisit to the budget. Revising the budget over time keeps it real. "Extraordinary" budget items have a way of proving to be "ordinary" items over time. That big car repair expense, those extra visits to the doctor for physicals so the kids can play sports, the trips back East to see an ailing parent—these are items that look "extraordinary," but in fact there are items like this every year! They're not extraordinary at all, just unplanned for. Thus, periodic updating and review are good. Then you let go.

POST SCRIPT ON LETTING GO

Because you are emotional (come on, don't wince—this is not a bad thing), you are inclined to feel a lot of vibrations around your personal family money. This is not fated. This is not wiring. This is something that can actually be cut—by you. Your real strengths lie in other parts of your life. Your relationships for one. Your informed judgment for two. Develop them, and extend out. Make more money, more art, more birdies, more compassion, more love, more medicine, or more wise-ass remarks. But your personal money world should be quite simple: set it in motion, periodically tend to the groove, heed that early warning system, and think personal money as little as you can. Isn't it time?

LOVE IN THE TIME OF PROSPERITY—PART III

The-Creative-in-Marriage is a hefty topic in its own right, and obviously part of the issue regards the ZM Type of the partner. The quick and dirty is: go with the brilliance of the partner's Type (i.e., to plan, to implement). For example, my wife is a true Maven. She loves a deal and jokes that she is "genuine Yankee frugal." Wheeling and dealing are sport for her. I myself have little interest in being around when she is doing her Maven thing, but I love the benefit of it.

However, my wife, like me, is not wired with the design mojo of The Architect, so it is strongly contraindicated for us to have planning sorts of discussions. Thus, if we want to buy a new car or are trying to figure out how much we can allocate to our oldest child's trip to Germany or we want to change something substantial in our budget, such as our clothing allowance, we do not as a rule discuss this by ourselves. This invites emotionality and misunderstanding. There is no planner "energy" in the room. We share the same planning blindspot. The Money Mandala is not complete.

Sure, we can talk in general terms (*yes, I'd like a SAAB 9-3; no, I don't want our son to fly business class*), but basically we gather our list and my bride makes a time to speak with our financial guy, Jared. If need be, I send an email or call Jared to provide input, express how important the matter is to me, and hear his initial thoughts. Then counselor (Jared) and Maven (my wife) come up with the best course of action, and I (The Creative) sign off on it. This process works. It's not the quickest, but it works swimmingly compared to the stressful alternatives. Stepping on the tail of the tiger is easy to do when you share a blindspot. Fortunately, Money Mandala keeps the peace, and that, at least in my book, never goes out of style.

NEVER FORGET MILES (AND THE BIRTH OF THE COOL)

It is understandable that you, The Creative, might have an initial freak-out at your ZM identity, exacerbated by society's harsh judgment. Moreover, you might cringe at all the interdependence issues. You need others. This can be intense. If your marriage is already on the fritz, and your spouse is The Archer— well, it's time to find your people fast, and get a good lawyer. But if it's not, then remember this: you are wired for relationships in the Hearth Money realm, and that's cool.

At some point the struggle abates. Your view of self and money shifts, once and for all, and you're free. A great burden is swept down river, like ice in springtime. *Yes, I have glitches with regards to all this personal money stuff. And in the immortal notes of Miles Davis:* **So What!** *It's Thursday afternoon, time to procure my weekly allowance, and away I go. First to the café for a pot of strong tea. Then on to Bart's CD Cellar, in search of some new ideas for the music blog. It's alter-ego time. It's time to live the dream. Meanwhile, my Money Mandala cats have got my back. Ciao!* Fair enough. Just remember Miles, OK? Be cool. That's right. Just let it go, and take control, grooving and ruling as the yin sovereign.

LISTS FOR LIST PEOPLE: THE CREATIVE ZM TYPE

FOCUS OF FINANCIAL PLANNING FOR THE CREATIVE TYPE:

1) Gather your people = your Mandala: bookkeeper, admin. assistant, financial planner, accountant, friend, spouse, parent, sister, business school student; one or two folks could suffice for most of it; communicate your objectives and focus.

2) Create a believable and current budget (based on recent spending patterns).

3) Shed light on critical blindspot areas (long-term care plan for parents or self, life insurance, asset protection, etc.).

4) Establish financial objectives (short, intermediate, and long term goals).

5) Commit to revising budget over time (Note: "extraordinary" line items have a way of proving to be "ordinary;" let's get them in the budget).

6) Establish a tracking system, and activate personnel to download info and keep it all current.

7) Establish planning priorities, with accompanying timetables.

8) Commit to revisiting and revising priorities (upkeeping, upgrading).

9) Compose Investment Policy Statement: proper risk/reward universe identified (done with investment advisor), based on your risk tolerance as well as your required return on investment. General rule of thumb: take on as little risk as possible to

accomplish your financial goals. Sleep well at night.

10) A to Z: Agree to make no major financial decisions by yourself. Work the circuit of the Mandala. Then your decisions will be well informed.

FOCUS OF IMPLEMENTATION FOR THE CREATIVE TYPE:

1) Get someone else to buy the car, once you and your planner friend have sussed out precisely what to buy. If that's not an option, then it's never a bad idea to gain the advice of Mavens before you buy anything. Also, it's OK to be discerning about Mavens themselves. Not all are created equal. Nor do they all share your tastes.

2) Work with a financial professional who is a skilled implementer (as was stated in The Architect's Money Mandala). That is, work with someone who not only knows best in class with regards to investments, but someone who works all the things around your money—investment expenses, tax efficiencies, coordination, and communication with the other people (for example, the accountant) in your Mandala.

3) As noted: take the emotion out of investing. "Buying into the plan" means letting go and letting the implementers freely implement within the scope of the investment plan. The Investment Policy Statement serves this end.

4) You need information formatted in a way that speaks to you. It MUST speak to you. Otherwise, have it reformatted: to graphs, bar charts, scatter charts, till you can SEE. "Executive summary" information is ideal. These reports need not be presentations

brimming with detail. Their function is to show that:

   a) you have made some money (income)

   b) you lived at a certain lifestyle (expense)

   c) there has been surplus (ideally)

   d) the other surplus monies (investments) are performing in accordance with the Investment Policy Statement and the overall markets

   Note: Periodic reports would do well to include: budget-to-actuals (Quicken is pretty easy), family balance sheet (Quicken, Excel), executive summary on investments (most likely Excel).

5) Delegate (as much as you can) the everyday management of personal finances. This could be to a smart young college person; a smart retired older person; bookkeeper, spouse, and so forth. Your check writing/credit card system is critical. Take a weekly allowance (the one in the plan), and keep everything else simple. Stay out of pretty much everything, if you can. A mail-opening, bill-pay service is ideal for some. That can be expensive. Can also go in the "best money ever spent" category. That being said, it's generally ill-advised to have someone else (spouse excepting) be signer on that account. Too dangerous. But you can certainly get your mail organized and checks periodically prepared, and all you have to do is review and sign.

6) Monitor and evaluate, and that includes yourself. Whether there are deviations from the budget, or things are spot on, the Money Mandala's objective is to hold up the mirror for you, The Creative. From time to time, you need to see yourself. You need to evaluate whether things are headed in the right direction. Your Money Mandala is there to assist with this: *No, it's not wise to purchase another Harley right now. No, you are between jobs, and now is not the time to use your free time and money reserves to do*

an extensive remodel. Yes, this is the exact moment to spend lavishly—it's your daughter's wedding and you've got the money!

7) Bless the Money Mandala. Your people are there for you. You've chosen them. If someone's not working out, then make the change. Beyond that, be the yin sovereign. Connect, gather, decide, let go. And live.

Chapter 17

THE ARCHER'S MONEY MANDALA

T HE ARCHER IS THE ZM Type that most personal financial books want to turn you into. What's more, she is of that self-selecting group that loves to rifle through the how-to articles and manuals of personal finance. How much of that information-gathering and advice-garnering she in fact needs remains to be seen. Some of it keeps her learning and growing, and this gives her levity. Much of it is exercise for the mind, and this keeps her sharp. She has a keen eye, Diana. She is masterful on a multitude of levels. Cool and calculating, she moves quietly through her world, processing great quantities of information from within herself and her environment, refreshing and renewing what is important to her, updating information about markets and marketplace; all of which lead to her inimitable sense of timing, of when to strike, of when to drop it and keep moving. But of the many fascinating qualities of The Archer, one is sly: this poster-child does not necessarily match the picture in your mind's eye of what The Archer should look like.

There are a lot of faux-Archers out there, walking around. Earlier on, I noted how numerous players in the financial services world are Creative ZM Types. They wear wire-rimmed glasses and in summer wear loafers with no socks and exude richness from every pore while drinking martinis at the club. But they're Archer imposters! Some are future candidates to act out John Cheever's "The Swimmer," which starts out as a hoot and turns slightly obnoxious and then ends ugly. OK, maybe I'm being dramatic. Then again, maybe not. But looking like The Archer and being The Archer are two entirely different things.

Melissa is a case in point. She lives with her beloved in a small house, right out of the Black Forest of the Grimms' Fairy Tales. Melissa has a lively artistic mind that pierces the ethers for all sorts of unexpected knowledge, and she is inclined to say wild things. She is a psychic, astrologist, artist of various media, and an Archer. Her goal in life is not to make scads of money. She's not quaffing cocktails at the club. Rather her value set is in line with being a high priestess of the intuitive and creative arts.

Her flouncy sprawling costumes, accessorized with layered necklaces of bead and stone and crystal, and a shawl for flipping and punctuating story or wild thought: All this does not a poster-child make!

And yet she is The Archer, who at the age of 55 took charge when her Dad died and Mom was overwhelmed, and then proceeded to do the same in her own immediate family. At once, her personal financial work was productive. This amazed her. *I had no idea I had THIS in me, though I still find it daunting.* Other ZM Types work such a situation and get mixed results. Not so for Melissa, who added personal money responsibility to a world resplendent with soul and intuition and creativity. Sometimes looks can be deceiving, even to a psychic.

NOTES ON MONEY MANDALA RX
FOR THE ARCHER ZM TYPE

FIRST AND FOREMOST

The arrows in the quiver, the bow, the sharp eye, the uncanny sense of time and place—these are your gifts. With them come rewards and responsibility. You are The Archer. Awakening to this truth is up to you, and you alone.

SOVEREIGN—TWO YANGS MAKE A YIN?

Planning is yang. Implementation is yang. And yet your sovereignty is yin. OK, no tricks here. Let's break this down. Planning is active (yang). You can do this for yourself, your family, and so on. Implementation is yang. This too you can do and do swimmingly.

Now for the yin sovereign piece. All this means is that it's fine for you to be actively, intimately involved in the planning and the implementation—you should be intimately connected—but not so much that you get absorbed or weighed down by it. Be connected, know what's going on, then delegate (as it fits) to your Money Mandala. Delegate, and direct your Money Mandala.

Part of your potency, Archer-on-the-watch, is having your hands free and your eyes gazing up and out, taking it all in. Refining the big picture, shoring up vulnerabilities, seizing opportunities, understanding the details of the plan and implementation. This comes from alacrity and big ZM view. Yin sovereign ever holds the big ZM view. The Archer, like no other Type, can look relaxed, as if skating along, when nothing could be further from the truth.

SOVEREIGN II—WHAT SORT OF REIGN?

Excessive pride is poison that tastes good in the moment. The fallacy of overreaching is something that you, The Archer, may have to contend with, depending on how magnanimous or petty, kind or critical your reign is. Money is great, but life is so much bigger. Mastery of Hearth Money is simply mastery of Hearth Money. Not more, not less. Interestingly, women who have more money said, in a recent study, that they have better sex because of their wealth.[15] Well, that rocks, I suppose, but what about the question: Do they have better love? (Note: the wealthier men did not say that having more money equated to better sex; but that's enough of *Zen Money Blues* going tabloid!)

You, Dear Archer, are refined and subtle in the personal finance realm. Indeed, you're a cool customer. You don't miss much in the personal finance universe. But then there's this other, not so small matter. You can forget to look in the mirror. Can ignore the interior world of character and values. Can carry on without genuine self-reflection, and that is risky business. Success and wealth can serve as dangerous opiates here. And so the question is posed: You, The Archer, are immensely talented, but to what end?

The Creative will immediately get the import of the question. You, Dear Archer, on the other hand, may respond with something akin to "see you at the finish line." However, the question is bigger than money. This is why The Creative has the potential to be The Archer's best friend, the Merlin in your world. For mastering money is one thing. Mastering both money and non-money is The Cosmic Big Leagues. Being a lordly Archer is not automatic admission to that game.

LOVE IN THE TIME OF PROSPERITY—PART IV

Where money ends and non-money begins—this is a line not so easily identified by The Archer or The Maven. Your reign, however, depends on this. So does your relationship. A spouse who is underwhelming in every Hearth Money way, is not "doing this to you on purpose." Unless of course your spouse is, in fact, doing it to you on purpose, in which case finding a couples therapist might be in order! But that's a different, cynical story, best told by John Updike and his ilk. Instead, we wish love for you, young-couple-in-love-on-whom-the-future-depends. And, we wish wisdom for you, that you come to recognize the contours of the line separating money from non-money.

Your story begins with the playing of the *Zen Money Blues* anthem, albeit with a slight variation: Get your personal money rock-steady, then do your relationship some good. You can't heal the world, or really welcome little ones into your world if the two of you are not strong and harmonizing. The platitudes about not going to bed angry and keeping money out of the bedroom are true. Easier said than done. The first one takes unwavering commitment. The second takes commitment and skill and kindness. Kindness that goes way beyond judgment. It is the kindness of working with what is—ZM wiring.

You, Dear Young Archer, are wired to take the lead. Contempt, resentment, criticism and the like are wholly unnecessary. Welcome the other energies—money and non-money—that your sweetheart brings. Forgive his shortcomings regarding personal finance, though of course hold him accountable. And with that as the core, extend the generosity out, to your children and parents and others with whom you cross paths. If money inhabits the bedrooms and intimate chambers of your family's life, then cast it out. It's never too late to set things right. Your spirit and your judgment matter, Dear Archer.

Two Eyes Open

With your talents and your Hearth Money mandate come a great responsibility. Protection is a part of your sovereignty. Protection of the purse and protection of your family's psyche. When things get dangerously or insidiously out of balance, you know. You always know. And that is the time for you to muster. Muster fearlessness. Muster counsel. Muster your people. Half the battle of personal finance is not letting your family take its own financial life. I know that hardly sounds rousing, but it's true. Archers ward off danger, as well as optimize the wealth and resources of the family purse.

Money Mandala—Mandala of Thought-Partners

"Thought-partners" are never wrong for you, Dear Archer. The benefits come on various levels. Initially the thought-partners bring you education and mentorship. You drink in not only information, but how to process it, how to think, how to step back and look at things, how to play the game. Indeed, you are the consummate student. Learning about personal finance matters never grows old for you. Multiple points of view elevate your decision making process, rather than create "paralysis by analysis" (as can be the case with other ZM Types). Your ZM diet consists of quality information and perspective. Nothing but clear, mature experts will suffice.

Some counselor relationships will be situational, as with the attorney who reviews the real estate contract for the purchase of your home. You'll activate those relationships to a specific end. Others will be long-standing, as with the accountant and financial advisor. Those relationships of course include more than thought-partnering. Managing, supervising, implementing, and coordinating—these services support you, particularly when your people are forward-looking, anticipating you and the season. For example, what is needed for tax time is no mystery. Actually getting all that information gathered and formatted for your accountant is another matter. These are the small things that let you keep doing what you do best: now moving, now not moving; which is to say, quietly and consistently observing the financial goings-on.

PLANNER IN YOUR MONEY MANDALA

Dear Archer, there's only one of you! Life happens. Holidays happen. Challenging times happen. Nor will you be here forever. Having an additional person hold the family's big picture is not necessary, but perhaps prudent. Having another hold the "financial family memory" lightens your load, and keeps you disciplined and focused and accountable—to yourself above all others. Protecting against the blindspot, against the foolish mistake, against something that should have been anticipated and thus planned for, is as important to you as cutting-edge knowledge. This, you know: preserving your wealth is as important as growing it.

COOL AND COLD

You don't need others, Dear Archer, but be careful not to be cold. You are so good at personal money, it could go to your head, and your success could invite attack from unforeseen and unanticipated quarters. Just because you can get a great deal, doesn't always mean you take it. Many folks will perform duties on your behalf, and do it for a song—that is due to your charisma. Do not take advantage. Be just. Your good name matters. Managing perception matters. No, you can't live your life in a reactive state, fending off criticism that one day in the future may come at you. But people do talk. People do watch. Magnanimity doesn't have to be pure altruism. Nonetheless, in society, magnanimity protects you.

THE EDUCATION OF LITTLE ARCHER

If you, The Archer, start with a puella's view of planning, then your education and mentorship should cut to the chase. Prioritizing is your sword to wield, without some big emotional overlay. Cutting is what you do. Detachment is what you learn. Disciplined, you refine your plan. It's not a big deal. Ultimately, you have insight like no other into what you are losing AND what you are gaining by cutting. If you let everything grow wildly, then soon the roses and young trees will be choked by chickweed and burdock leaves and elm suckers. This is not good. Cut!

LEGACY

What will yours be? What seeds do you sow? How magnanimous is your rule? How will you be remembered?

LOVE IN THE TIME OF PROSPERITY—PART V

I don't care what others say: life does not get simpler as it goes on. Just ask Kimberly, Archer *par excellence*. She's marrying husband number three, and Ding! it's time to not only engage the legal counsel of Bernie the Pre-Nup Maestro, but also time to map out how family finances will be handled with Hubby #3 around. This is complicated.

Firstly, prenuptial agreements are notoriously breakable in the Sunshine State where she lives. You cannot be too careful. Kimberly knows this and seeks a second legal opinion, to have alongside

Bernie's. That second opinion is another five hundred bucks for an hour-and-twenty-minute meeting. That's all right. This is money well spent.

Kimberly is working it, leveraging the extensive case experience of her financial planner and two attorneys, regarding a truly critical and sensitive matter, because she has considerably more wherewithal than her septuagenarian fiancé. Kimberly wants things tidy, yet still romantic. A tall order! But she gets there. It seems that in the State of Florida, there is a way to fireproof (as best as is ever possible) the pre-nup. Simply put, the pre-nup needs to be signed six months in advance of the wedding ceremony. Then future hubby cannot plead "duress" (i.e., *I got pushed into doing this pre-nup right before the ceremony...um, OK, it was actually four months before we went to the Justice of the Peace, but it was soooo stressful the day I signed that pre-nup... Yep, that's my story and I'm sticking to it!*).

From there, Love In The Time of Prosperity gets better. Kimberly is able to breathe out and integrate a portion of her finances with those of her new husband. On one level, this is "just business," making use of the potentially unused portion of New Hubby's estate credit exemption. On another level, it is a good faith gesture to the relationship, as if to say: *I love you. I accept the risks inherent in that. Not everything is about me and my money. I want to honor that.* A Raven Maven might have destroyed the relationship over this.

Kimberly wanted a man, did not want to be alone with her riches in the afternoon of life, and did her Archer thing. She honored and acknowledged the "social contract" with her new husband, and she did it with integrity and intelligence and thorough due diligence. Now there is the not-so-small matter of love. *Bonne chance, Kimberly!*

INVESTMENTS—PLANNING AND IMPLEMENTATION

You plan like The Architect, you implement like The Maven, and you have The Archer's sixth sense. At this point you know the drill. But if you need a refresher, go to the investment sections of The Architect and The Maven. Otherwise keep the most basic Archer rule in mind:

Never abdicate your Archer throne. Ever.

LISTS FOR LIST PEOPLE: THE ARCHER ZM TYPE

FOCUS OF FINANCIAL PLANNING FOR THE ARCHER TYPE

1) You initially need education, coaching, mentoring. Then you can do-it-yourself and do it swimmingly.

2) Helpers are situational and often times temporary.

3) Engaging quality thought-partners is never wrong.

4) Proactive professionals generate tremendous value in your world, but again, you do not need them.

5) Just because you can, does not mean you automatically do. Each day is one of renewal and refocusing for you, The Archer. Seize that day, or risk losing your accuracy.

FOCUS OF IMPLEMENTATION FOR THE ARCHER TYPE:

1) You do well to be kind to others, generous with small things and generous with praise.

2) It behooves you to be magnanimous in your judgment of others. 90% of the folks (that includes your siblings, parents, spouse, children, and so on) do not and will not have your ZM chops. You can run circles around them, if you want to, though this probably isn't a good idea.

3) Be neither cold nor aloof. Almost as important, do not appear cold or aloof. Manage the perceptions of others. You are "the natural," once activated and educated. Your success may appear as luck or greed to others. Don't let these perceptions linger unattended. From time to time, it's OK to let others see you not get

the best deal.

4) Take care of your people. Be loyal and expect loyalty in turn. Invest in relationships of various shapes and sizes. There are layers of protection—social, psychological, financial—that others bring to the relationship. Be careful of isolation.

5) Be noble with your power. You are powerful in the land of Hearth Money.

Chapter 18 Adieu

RGUABLY, THE BEST COMMUNITIES of the next 300 years—the communities that rise above all others and influence the direction of society—will be the ones who can do money. Doing money begins with talking about it. Really talking about money. Getting down to the bones of it. These communities will not necessarily be the richest in terms of dollars and net worth. Rather, what they will have is the scent of cheerfulness and good will and affirmation around their money. They will know when to grow roots down into the earth and when to grow up and reach for the heavens. They will focus on the art of living, because they will already have their money thing right. Being resourceful is richness. Being energized in your marriage is richness. Seeing the children, all the children, thrive and learn and grow is richness. Being free to innovate and create in your professional life is richness. The approach of the great communities will not be accursed by the usual suspects. Myopia is bad luck. Growing too high too fast, without depth and stability—that equally is bad luck. Autopilot is bad luck. Diverging ZM Type styles with no Mandala to contain and maintain them is bad luck.

Money is wrapped in so many hopes and dreams, and prompts discourse that even weaves in our own mortality. Money runs through some dark canyons of the psyche and marriage and family and community. Thankfully, it doesn't end there. There is good news. The situation is knowable. The situation is workable. Self-knowledge goes a long way. Money Mandala means you can create a place where you, your family, and your community can shine a light on all sorts of critical matters, and do it in a way that enriches everyone. Freud said that money is as taboo as sex. No doubt this is true, but isn't that kind of strange? It's time this taboo ran its course.

Zen Money Typology is a start. To really talk about money, to really get down to the bones of it, and not be plagued by misunderstanding and emotionality and animus, there must be a shared language. Fresh language, born of that mythic village and shaped by the vernacular of these modern times. Respectful language, that includes every member of the community. I admit my bias here, which is of the *Lord of the Rings* variety: everyone, large or small, king or magician or hobbit, Architect or Maven or Creative or Archer, has her part to play in the great heroic story. It is a cosmic crime when someone misses the epic voyage because personal money stole her mind. We lose too, because there's one more person, insidiously distracted, who cannot possibly wholeheartedly offer her gifts to the community.

This is a complex world we live in. The demands of the culture of uber-individualism are vast, rigorous, and unreasonable. In fact, they're absurd, at least where personal money is concerned. For most of us, money is best a social experience. There is no shame in this. It's age old. It's a good thing. In these modern times, money has become the archetypal thief, taking advantage of us in our isolated state. However, we can see through this thief now. He's not substantial. Nor is he the real enemy. The enemy is us on autopilot. The Architect and The Maven can be a marriage made in ZM heaven, or become World War III. The dynamic between ZM Types can play out, sweetly or horrifically, between spouses or across family generations. Architect daughter and Maven mother have so much to offer each other. However, if one or both remain in autopilot mode, this will spell trouble. The Archer may indeed find her perfect soul mate in The Creative, but will their union survive dealings with personal money? The Tao is very clear about how to avoid conflict: clearly establish roles and responsibilities and expectations from the outset.[16] *Zen Money Blues* builds on that, but only thrives on the road of wakefulness, The Inner Highway 61. Few relationships will survive autopilot. Money is incendiary. Criticism and contempt, along with the stress of mismanagement, destroy relationships. The best communities of tomorrow won't let this happen. They won't let opportunity and material good fortune go dark, veering down one of any number of roads that lead to relationship bankruptcy. When needed, they'll invoke the spirit of Rinzai, and rouse the courage and compassion necessary to bring things back into balance. For life has its fair share of suffering imbedded in the very proposition of being alive: personal money, thank goodness, need not contribute to that.

FULL CIRCLE

We commenced our *Zen Money Blues* expedition with the legendary BB King. It was late April 2005, a sparkling N'Orleans day on the fairgrounds. The 79 year-old Master Bluesman was in ferocious form, chiding his musicians and insisting that everybody clap those hands and shake that soul. He was delivering the good news! Of course, no one knew that four months later the levees would break. No one knew that the crib of American culture would be underwater, that generations of musicians would scatter in the ten directions, and that anarchy would reign for a shamefully long time. But the inspiration of that Jazz Fest day remains the same. For all the things that we cannot control, there are many that we can do something about. Hearing and recounting the far-ranging stories, looking at and laughing at our miscues and blindspots, moving this activity from one of personal pain and isolation to a "social experience" that together we can discuss and put in its proper place—this is the inspiration of *Zen Money Blues*. This is blues. Blues is good. The sparkle of that N'Orleans day can never be diminished. The good news about your mind and your money is that all of this is workable. Let's get it right. Let's make our money world rock-steady, then go out and do the world some good. The planet's counting on us.

ENDNOTES

[1] Sigmund Freud, *Collected Papers* (London: Hogarth Press, 1932).

[2] Webster's online dictionary can be found at: *http://www.merriam-webster.com/*.

[3] Robert Frost, "The Road Not Taken" (New York: Henry Holt, 1920).

[4] This quotation is from "Lady Windermere's Fan: A Play About a Good Woman," a four act comedy by Oscar Wilde, first produced at the St. James Theatre in London in 1892 (first published in 1893). Typical of Wilde, this comedy is a biting satire on the morals of the Victorian era marriage.

[5] English rock group, Led Zeppelin, released its arrangement of "In My Time of Dying" on their *Physical Graffiti* album on February 24, 1975, on their own Swan Song Records label. It was arranged by Jimmy Page, Robert Plant, John Paul Jones, and John Bonham. "In My Time of Dying" is a traditional blues song that has been covered by numerous rock musicians since the early 1960's. The first known recording of this song had the title "Jesus Make Up My Dying Bed" and was recorded by blues-gospel guitarist Blind Willie Johnson between 1927 and 1930.

[6] Richard Wilhelm Translation/Cary F. Banes (Trans. into English), *The I Ching or Book of Changes* (New Jersey: Princeton University Press, 1977), pp. 111-114, from the 28th hexagram, "Preponderance of the Great."

[7] Ernest Hemmingway, *The Sun Also Rises* (New York: Scribner Paperback Fiction, Simon & Schuster Inc., 1926), p. 141.

[8] Richard Wilhelm Translation/Cary F. Banes (Trans. into English), *The I Ching or Book of Changes* (New Jersey: Princeton University Press, 1977), pp. 28-31, from the 6th hexagram, "Conflict."

[9] Sources on the virtues of passive investing are: *Winning the Loser's Game: Timeless Strategies for Successful Investing* by Charles Ellis (New York: McGraw-Hill, 1998); "Improved Study Finds Index Management Usually Outperforms Active Management" by Millicent Holmes (*Journal of Financial Planning*, January 2007); The Vanguard Group, Inc. and Lipper, Inc. (two companies that provide information and data).

[10] This phenomenon is well documented on *Morningstar.com*, under "Investor Returns," again in Charles Ellis' book *Winning the Loser's Game* (see #9), and in "Getting More of What the Markets Give" (*The Wall Street Journal*, January 21, 2007).

[11] This widely used expression was coined by Thomas L. Friedman in his book, *The World Is Flat: A Brief History of the Twenty-first Century* (New York: Farrar, Straus and Giroux, 2005).

[12] Richard Florida, *The Rise of the Creative Class: And How It's Transforming Work, Leisure, Community and Everyday Life* (New York: Basic Books, 2002).

[13] Maurice Sendak, *Pierre: A Cautionary Tale in Five Chapters and a Prologue* (New York: HarperCollins Publishers, Inc., 1962).

[14] Richard Wilhelm Translation/Cary F. Banes (Trans. into English), *The I Ching or Book of Changes* (New Jersey: Princeton University Press, 1977), p. 60, from the 14th hexagram, "Possession in Great Measure."

[15] Thomas Kostigen, "More Money, Better Sex" (*Marketwatch.com*, January 30, 2007).

[16] Richard Wilhelm Translation/Cary F. Banes (Trans. into English), *The I Ching or Book of Changes* (New Jersey: Princeton University Press, 1977), pp. 28-31.

BIBLIOGRAPHY

Ellis, Charles. *Winning the Loser's Game: Timeless Strategies for Successful Investing.* New York: McGraw-Hill, 1998.

Gladwell, Malcolm. *The Tipping Point: How Little Things Can Make a Big Difference.* New York: Little, Brown and Company, 2000.

Jung, Carl G. *Mandala Symbolism.* Translated by R.F.C. Hull. New Jersey: Princeton University Press, 1959.

Jung, Carl G. *Modern Man in Search of a Soul.* Translated by W.S. Dell and Cary F. Baynes. New York: Harcourt, Inc., 1933.

Jung, Carl G. *Psychological Types.* A revision by R.F.C. Hull of the translation by H.G. Baynes. New Jersey: Princeton University Press, 1971.

Swenson, David F. *Unconventional Success: A Fundamental Approach to Personal Investment.* New York: Free Press, A Division of Simon & Schuster, Inc., 2005.

Watson, Burton. *Zen Teachings of Master Lin-Chi: A Translation of the Lin-chi lu.* New York: Columbia University Press, 1999.

Wilhelm, Richard (Translator), Baynes, Cary F. (translation into English). *The I Ching or Book of Changes.* New Jersey: Princeton University Press, 1977.

ACKNOWLEDGEMENTS

I wish to thank my editorial team of Barry Boyce, Carolyn Kanjuro, and Maria Butler. They were patient, impeccable, and assiduous throughout.

Appreciation and acknowledgement also go to Wells Christie, Susan Edwards, Denny Robertson, and Gregge Tiffen, with whom there were lively, seminal conversations dating back to the late 90's. In particular, Gregge had his own original ideas about the dual nature of money, while Denny went on to develop her own version of the planner/implementer matrix.

Thank you to Mikyo for his fierce, caring, accurate copy-edit of the book; and to the mercurial Mark Resnick, who was a truly generous and gritty thought-partner start to finish.

Finally, I should like to express sincere gratitude to my book designer, Michael Signorella. Tasteful, thoughtful, and kind, he offered invaluable suggestions that genuinely upgraded the final product.

ABOUT THE AUTHOR

 *Zen Money Blues* is a project ten years in the making, reflective of Mark Butler's long-standing love for dharma, psychology, family, music, writing, and, of course, personal finance. His firm, Butler Financial, provides independent investment counsel and financial planning. Boulder, Colorado is home for Mark and his family.

LaVergne, TN USA
30 October 2010
202873LV00001B/2/P